HOW SCAPEGOATS CAN HEAL FROM NARCISSISTIC ABUSE

3 Steps Towards Compassion, Protection & Freedom.

JAY REID, LPCC

Copyright © 2023 by Jay Reid

All rights reserved. No part of this publication may be reproduced, stored in any form of retrieval system or transmitted in any form or by any means without prior permission in writing from the publishers except for the use of brief quotations in a book review.

Published in the United States of America

Dedication

This book is dedicated to fellow scapegoat survivors of narcissistic parents fighting for empowerment.

I want to thank my sister, Jessica, for her steadfast support, courage, and love.

Contents

Dedication iii

Contents iv

Chapter 1: The Narcissistic Parent's 'Hot Potato' Of Worthlessness 13

    How the parent passes the hot potato to the scapegoat child 13

    Why the parent needs the child to hold the potato 15

    Why the scapegoat child holds the potato 16

    The scapegoat child's life with the parent's potato 17

    Why a scapegoat keeps holding the potato of worthlessness into adulthood 18

    Moving to a world where you can safely drop the potato 19

    Working with a therapist 22

Chapter 2: The scapegoat child's world 23

    How a narcissistic parent organizes their reality 23

    When a child enters the world of a narcissistic parent 33

    The narcissistic parent's solution: Scapegoat their child 36

    Impacts on the scapegoat child 39

Chapter 3: The scapegoat child's role & symptoms in narcissistic abuse 40

    How the scapegoat role develops 41

    Functions of the scapegoat child's role 42

    How the child participates as the scapegoat 42

    The scapegoat child's symptoms 45

Chapter 4: Two ways a scapegoat survivor keeps their narcissistic parent around 47

    Our early worlds are shaped by the people in it - for better or worse 48

When closeness to a parent means suffering ... 49

Two ways a scapegoat child stays close to their internalized narcissistic parent ... 50

Treating yourself the way your narcissistic parent treated you ... 50

Living as if your narcissistic parent is still around and in charge ... 52

Pillar #1: Making Sense of What Happened (So You Know It Was Not Your Fault) ... 56

Chapter 5: Making sense of what happened with the first Pillar of Recovery ... 57

The scapegoat child must accept their parent's abuse ... 57

The narcissistic parent has a privileged status in the scapegoat child's mind ... 58

The narcissistic parent's ongoing influence in the scapegoat survivor's life ... 59

How Pillar #1 helps scapegoat survivors build a new frame of reference ... 62

Thinking about the internalized narcissistic parent ... 64

Chapter 6: Be the scapegoat or be nobody to no one ... 65

The child's need to find themselves in their parent's mind ... 66

The conditions of being found in the narcissistic parent's mind ... 66

The threat of being nobody to no one ... 69

Coping with this threat today ... 70

Chapter 7: Neither the scapegoat nor golden child wins in narcissistic abuse ... 72

Why a narcissistic parent creates the scapegoat & golden child ... 73

The costs to the children in these roles ... 74

How the scapegoat and golden child roles are pitted against each other ... 78

Possibilities for reconciliation 80

The laissez-faire principle 81

Chapter 8: Three Ways The Narcissistic Parent Blocks The Scapegoat Child's Growth 84

Narcissistic parents exploit their children 84

Three ways the narcissistic parent interrupts the scapegoat child's growth 86

How to resume growth 91

Chapter 9: Invisible to a narcissistic parent 92

3 ways children feel invisible to the narcissistic parent 93

How children survive by living narrowly 96

Relationships where you are visible 99

Chapter 10: When the scapegoat has to deny their own gifts 102

The dangers of the scapegoat child owning their gifts 103

How the scapegoat child copes 106

How scapegoat survivors continue denying their gifts 107

The path to recovering your gifts 108

Chapter 11: Fear of growing up for scapegoat survivors of narcissistic parents 110

The narcissistic parent's need to domineer their child 111

Why submission is the only option for the scapegoat child 112

The threat of the child's growth to the narcissistic parent 114

The scapegoat child's beliefs that interfere with growing up .. 115

Recovery involves picking up your adult self from storage 118

Recovery through therapy 119

Chapter 12: When scapegoats escape inward to survive narcissistic abuse 123

When there's nobody to consistently connect to 124

How does this affect the scapegoat survivor as an adult? .. 126

What can be done? 127

Chapter 13: When scapegoat survivors think: "It's only me finds who this difficult" 128

    Challenges make the scapegoat child feel inferior, strange & alone 129

    How the scapegoat child is made to feel inferior in the face of challenges 129

    A strategy to feel adequate, normal and connected in the face of challenges 134

    An exercise to de-stigmatize feeling challenged 136

Chapter 14: Four reasons the scapegoat child is stronger than their narcissistic parent 138

    Being more powerful does not equal strength 139

    Give yourself the credit you are due 148

Chapter 15: Self-consciousness in scapegoat survivors of narcissistic abuse 149

    Why a narcissistic parent makes a scapegoat child feel self-conscious 150

    What life is like for the scapegoat child 152

    How to escape the binds of self-consciousness 155

Chapter 16: How the scapegoat survivor may confuse badness with realness 159

    How the scapegoat child is led to confuse badness with realness 160

    The siren song of catharsis for the scapegoat survivor 162

    Finding what is good and real in yourself 164

Chapter 17: When getting better feels like 'selling out' after narcissistic abuse 167

    Narcissistic abuse that is - supposedly - for your own good 168

    Limit the narcissistic parent's wrath by any means necessary 169

The aftermath: Resurrecting your resentment 172

Recovery: Relocating the betrayal from within to without 174

Chapter 18: When learning about narcissism stops being helpful 177

At long last: The first dose of information about narcissism 178

How learning about narcissism may go too far 180

The other two ingredients to healing 182

Pillar #2: Gaining Distance from Narcissistic Abusers (and Closeness to Safe People) 186

Chapter 19: Choosing and protecting safe relationships with the second Pillar of Recovery 187

How staying close to the internalized narcissistic parent protects the scapegoat child 189

Abandoned 189

Anguished 190

Astray 191

The challenge of the second pillar 192

The promise of the second pillar 193

What to expect in this section 194

Chapter 20: A tell-tale sign of safe people for scapegoat survivors of narcissistic parents 195

Having to fill your narcissistic parent's emptiness 196

How life feels when others' happiness takes priority 197

Grant yourself permission to center your happiness 199

5 signs of a safe relationship 200

Chapter 21: The science behind gaining distance from the narcissistic abuser 202

How do our nervous systems determine if we are safe or not? 204

Applying the polyvagal theory to recovery from narcissistic abuse 205

Chapter 22: Restoring your boundaries after narcissistic intrusions 208
    The narcissistic parent's 'right' to intrude 209
    The scapegoat child's dilemma 211
    The scapegoat child's solution 212
    Recovering your boundaries 214

Chapter 23: Closeness without confinement after narcissistic abuse 218
    2 components that lead to empowered closeness 219
    Overcoming what closeness used to mean 222
    What closeness can mean now 223

Chapter 24: Heal from narcissistic abuse by taking others' support for granted 226
    A narcissistic parent blocks the scapegoat child's healthy entitlement 227
    The impact on the scapegoat child 230
    Recover your right to take others for granted 231

Pillar #3: Defy the Narcissist's Rules 233

Chapter 25: Defying the narcissist's rules with the third Pillar of Recovery 234
    Staying close to your internalized narcissistic parent forbids feeling good 236
    Two ways scapegoat survivors prevent themselves from feeling good 239
    The third Pillar makes it safe to feel good 241

Chapter 26: Take off the scapegoat nametag at the narcissistic family's conference 243
    The narcissistic family conference 244
    Leaving the conference 245
    Ripping off the scapegoat nametag 245

Chapter 27: Living in the first person after narcissistic abuse 247

The threats posed by the narcissistic parent 248

The scapegoat child's "solution" to stay with the narcissistic parent 249

5 impacts of this "solution" on the scapegoat survivor 251

How therapy can help the scapegoat survivor live in the first person 253

Ways to live in the first person outside of therapy 255

Chapter 28: Recovering honesty after narcissistic abuse 256

The danger of honesty with a narcissistic parent 257

How a child avoids this danger: Distortion 257

The costs of distortion for the child 259

The path to safe honesty 262

Chapter 29: Realistic self-worth for scapegoat survivors 266

How the scapegoat child creates secret and perfectionistic self-worth 267

The necessity of secrecy 267

The resulting flimsiness of the scapegoat child's self-worth 268

Forming a shared and realistic basis for self-worth 270

The secret to building realistic self-worth: There is no secret! 271

Making your secret self-worth known to others 272

Chapter 30: Healing a shame-based identity for scapegoat survivors 274

Hiding the narcissistic parent's sins in the scapegoat child 275

The scapegoat child's resulting shame-based identity 278

Excavating shame from the scapegoat survivor's identity 280

Chapter 31: Recovering desire for scapegoat survivors of narcissistic abuse 283

The problem that desire creates for the scapegoat child 284

3 ways the child is pressured to surrender desire 285

• x •

The agony of thwarted desire for the scapegoat child 286

How to recover desire 288

Chapter 32: Heal from fear of persecution for scapegoat
survivors of narcissistic parents 291

How the scapegoat child gets persecuted 292

How the scapegoat survivor protects from further
persecution 293

The dilemma of healing 294

Chapter 33: The Challenge of Creativity for Scapegoat
Survivors of Narcissistic Parents 297

The dilemma of the creative scapegoat survivor 298

3 punishments for the scapegoat child's creativity 300

How scapegoat survivors can find it safe to be creative 303

Finding creative outlets 305

Chapter 34: Defy the narcissistic rule that love means being
helped up 306

When a parent can't stand their own imperfection 307

The child's (lack of) options 309

Impacts of having to equate love with help on the child 310

Moving from needing to exchanging help 313

Chapter 35: How the scapegoat survivor can recover faith in
themselves 316

How the scapegoat child uses their parts to fit in 317

An IFS map of jamal's inner world 319

Distinguishing the parts from their burdens 320

References 323

1

The Narcissistic Parent's 'Hot Potato' Of Worthlessness

I have fond memories of rainy days as a second grader. Instead of playing outside for recess, we had to stay indoors. My teacher would arrange our chairs in a circle. One kid held a beanbag that was the 'hot potato.' The teacher would start playing a song, and we would pass the bean bag around the circle. The kid holding the 'hot potato' was out of the game when the music stopped. No one wanted to be holding the hot potato at that point.

A narcissistic parent does not feel good about themselves at their core. Instead of taking responsibility for these feelings they play a rigged game of hot potato with their child. They get to be a player of the game *and* the one in control of the music. They pass the hot potato of worthlessness to the child then shut the music off. The child stuck with the potato is that parent's scapegoat.

How the parent passes the hot potato to the scapegoat child

A narcissistic parent uses a subtle yet convincing psychological maneuver to pass the potato. There are three steps:

1) unconsciously relocate their own feelings of worthlessness into their child,
2) devalue, deprive, and control the child into thinking and feeling they are worthless, and
3) enjoy a false sense of superiority at the expense of this child.

This maneuver is called pathological projective identification (Reid & Kealy, 2022). It protects the parent from the hot potato of worthlessness. They go from being helpless in the face of these feelings to the one in control. So long as they can keep the child holding this hot potato the parent is safe from it.

The child in this position is called the 'scapegoat'. They are emotionally deprived, devalued, and controlled by the parent. Treating the child this way convinces both parties that it is the child who is worthless - not the parent.

For this to work the narcissistic parent needs their child to keep playing the game. Tragically the child has no choice but to do so.

For as long as she could remember, Samantha felt like her mother's enemy[1]. She never knew what she did to deserve such animosity. What she did know is that every interaction with her mother would result in Samantha getting blamed for something. At meals, she would be criticized for not having table manners worthy of the Royal Family. She was chewing too loudly, her elbows

---

[1] All case examples in this book are anonymized composite examples drawn from the author's clinical, personal, and professional experience.

> were on the table, she was eating too fast, and/or she was not eating enough.
>
> Her mother would find fault with Samantha's decisions in her life. She doubted Samantha's ability to be polite to others and would monitor her behavior in public. Later, she would assail Samantha with accusations that she acted improperly. If Samantha brought home a report card with good grades, her mother would accuse her of laziness for any grade less than an A+.
>
> Samantha could do nothing right in her mother's eyes. Since she had no other frame of reference, she trusted her mother's assessment of her. She must be prone to bad manners, impoliteness, and laziness. Her mother was doing her the "favor" of pointing out these flaws so that Samantha might fix them.

Why the parent needs the child to hold the potato

A narcissistic parent needs this child as much as they supposedly revile them. To feel in control of their own worthless feelings they need to experience those feelings as belonging to the child and know they can make the child feel this way. The child must keep holding the potato for the parent to do this.

> What Samantha could not have known about her mother was how easily she could feel worthless. Her mother created a conscious identity where she was entitled to be in charge of others, and by extension, she

felt superior to them. But this conscious identity was a rickety band-aid over a core sense of worthlessness that was impossible to shake.

Her mother saw Samantha's natural propensity to enjoy life and be kind to others and grew envious. Seeing Samantha possess what she did not made her want to ruin these qualities in Samantha. She felt worthless for lacking what Samantha had and would make Samantha pay. This was why she made it her mission to find fault in nearly everything Samantha said or did.

Samantha's buoyancy and vitality diminished over time. She could not sustain them in the face of her mother's constant criticism. Instead, she felt worthless. Now, her mother felt less threatened by Samantha. Samantha's lack of vitality meant her mother had less to envy.

Why the scapegoat child holds the potato

It is worse for the scapegoat child to drop the potato than to hold on. The rigged game of hot potato is the only world the child is offered by their narcissistic parent. In order for a child to feel like they exist they must find themselves in that world.

The narcissistic parent will punish the child for deviating from the role of scapegoat. Shows of prowess or pride are met with doubt and skepticism by the parent. Being met this way when the child hopes for reinforcement produces toxic levels of shame. The scapegoat child learns that there is no place in their world with the parent where the child's value is legitimate.

The scapegoat child's life with the parent's potato

Life is grim and constricted for a scapegoat child. They must anchor themselves in a world that insists on their worthlessness. This means they cannot overtly grow into the people they were born to be.

The scapegoat child's potentials become hazards rather than assets. Capabilities threaten their ability to identify as worthless. So, the child must unconsciously adopt beliefs that keep them in denial about their worth. Here are a few:

"If I am not being productive, then I am worthless."

"I do not deserve protection."

"I am defective."

"I am unattractive."

"I am always one mistake away from complete ruin."

"Others' needs are more important than my own."

Such beliefs make success and worth feel fraudulent to the scapegoat child.

> *Samantha found herself denying her strengths. She was a naturally good painter. She could see what she wanted to paint in her mind's eye and bring that picture to life on paper. In eighth grade, her art teacher, Ms. Simonis, took note of Samantha's talent. One day after class, she*

asked Samantha to stay behind and told her, "You really have a gift. I hope you continue to work at this."

Samantha felt a bewildering mix of ecstasy, pride and terror. She did not know why a compliment would feel so scary but it did. The next day in class, Samantha started acting up in ways she had never done before. She threw things at the chalkboard when Ms. Simonis turned towards it. She spoke loudly to her friend sitting across the room. All of this forced Ms. Simonis to discipline Samantha by giving her a detention. From then on, Samantha would find it impossible to focus and paint in the ways she used to.

Samantha had to adopt the belief that she was defective. Ms. Simonis's positive feedback on her painting was at odds with this belief and threatened Samantha's membership in her mother's world. She had to thwart Ms. Simonis's positive impression of her to stay psychologically safe.

Why a scapegoat keeps holding the potato of worthlessness into adulthood

The scapegoat child grew up in the only world available to share with their family. As painful as this was, it grew to be familiar. It was far better than having no world to share with the people closest to them. Chapter 2 examines the psychology of the narcissistic parent so you understand what you had to contend with as a child. Chapter 3 describes how such parents builds the scapegoat child's world.

We do not easily swap out the world we grew up in for a different world. In fact, the more abusive our early world was the more tightly we cling to it (Celani, 2011). This is why scapegoat survivors find it so difficult to 'think positively about themselves' despite having loads of insight into the origins of why they see themselves as defective and undeserving. Until a new world is experientially available it is impossible to live differently. Chapter 4 explains what keeps the scapegoat child and survivor in the world of their narcissistic parent.

This begs the question: How does a scapegoat survivor build a new world for themselves? A world where they deserve compassion, protection, and freedom?

Moving to a world where you can safely drop the potato

I developed the concept of the Three Pillars of Recovery to explain how scapegoat survivors discover such a world for themselves. These pillars work together to create new experiences of compassion, protection, and freedom.

Pillar #1: Making sense of what happened

The scapegoat child must convince themselves of their worthlessness to stay in their parent's world. They reason that their parent deprives, devalues, and controls them because they do not deserve better. Now the parent is just treating the child like the bad person they –

supposedly - are. The narcissistic parent's abuse may even be seen as a virtuous effort to fix the child's badness.

This pillar of recovery involves learning about pathological narcissism to realize that you were *undeservedly* abused. Instead of seeing your childhood as evidence of your defectiveness or undeservedness, you get to see how it was rigged against you. As you reflect on your past in this new light compassion for yourself emerges.

Chapters 5 through 18 show you that you never chose to hold your parent's hot potato of worthlessness. You will see how your ability to survive such circumstances deserves admiration.

Pillar #2: Move away from narcissistic abusers & towards safe people

In order to move to a new world where you are safe to know your worth you need distance from narcissistic abusers. Being close to people who deprive, devalue, and control you today reinforces the lessons from the old world. Such people will punish you for the "offense" of living from a sense of deservedness and adequacy. This pillar helps you offer yourself protection for your emotional well-being from threats today.

Chapters 19 to 25 guide you toward people who do not play the game of hot potato. You will learn the science that supports the need for distance from narcissistic abusers. You will learn how and why you may feel guilt and fear when creating such distance. And you will learn tactics to overcome these obstacles.

Pillar #3: Live in defiance of the narcissist's rules

A critical ingredient of building this new world is the experience of safety when you defy your narcissistic parent's rules. This means deliberately choosing and acting in ways that reflect your worth and adequacy. You gain experience that nothing terrible happens when you are good to yourself. As you accrue more and more such experiences, you find the freedom to choose and act in ways that align with your own rules.

Chapters 26 to 36 show how to leave the game of hot potato altogether. The world you are building for yourself runs on a different sort of fuel than the old world. You are not running on self-criticism to secure your place in this world. Instead you are running on pride and dignity while seeing that these experiences secure your existence in this new world.

> *Samantha attended college away from home and took a job as a business analyst. Although she demonstrated competency in this role she shrunk from sharing her point of view in meetings. She would share her findings with her manager and ask him to be the one to share at an upcoming meeting. Whenever Samantha spoke up at work she was flooded with fear and shame. At her first performance review she got high marks for her*

productivity. However her manager told her, "Look, Samantha, you have a bright future here but you need to grow more comfortable speaking up. Your perspective is well-informed and valuable. People in the company need to see this about you."

Samantha knew she needed help if she was to put her manager's feedback into practice. So, she looked up 'difficulty speaking up in meetings' and eventually found some YouTube videos that linked this to growing up with a narcissistic parent. These videos emphasized the importance of getting into therapy and so Samantha booked her first appointment. Thus began her journey towards building a new world for herself that ran on self-worth instead of self-diminishment.

Working with a therapist

This book is meant to supplement – rather than replace – your work in therapy to recover from this form of abuse. The prospect of therapy may seem scary to some scapegoat survivors, given what closeness to others has meant in the past. As scary as therapy may seem, it is also how the most profound wounds from narcissistic abuse get healed. Scapegoat survivors need new, experience in safe relationships where they are free to feel their worth without losing the other's connection to them. This was the opposite of what they experienced at the hands of their narcissistic parent. No book or instructional material can substitute for such needed experience.

2

The Scapegoat Child's World

> *Was your parent extremely sensitive to slights?*
> *Did they react with contempt and hostility towards*
> *you for minor mistakes?*
> *Did they treat other people much better than you?*

To understand the scapegoat child's origin we need to go back to before they were born. We need to understand the pathologically narcissistic personality of the parents that shape the child's world.

How a narcissistic parent organizes their reality

The patchwork approach to self-worth

A narcissistic parent finds it very difficult to maintain realistic self-esteem (Weinberg & Ronningstam, 2022). They rely on continual affirmation and admiration from others to pastiche together an exaggerated sense of worth. They believe they are and deserve to be more important than others (Krizan & Herlache, 2018).

All of this manifests in the pursuit of higher status than others (Grapsas et al., 2020). The status pursuit in narcissism or SPIN model says they are motivated by status above all other motives.

Achieving the highest status trumps connection to others and reaching moral ideals. They will do whatever they can to boost themselves or devalue others. Either tactic raises their status. So long as they are convinced they hold the highest status then their self-worth stays intact.

> Samantha's mother was named Chavon. She had a difficult childhood where here parents were extremely status conscious. They took little interest in Chavon's inner life. They expected near perfection from her and she resolved at an early age to deliver.
>
> Whenever the family was together conversation was about the parent's accomplishments or Chavon's. Her mother would incessantly ask her if she had done her homework. She was continually skeptical of Chavon's ability to excel. Every time Chavon brought home an 'A' from school her mother acted surprised.
>
> Chavon had to keep her problems to herself. Her parents never seemed to have any problems so she better not. The only times she felt good was when she felt better than others. So, she resolved to do whatever it took to be superior.

What is beneath the patchwork?

The SPIN model explains how and why a narcissistic parent might insist on holding the highest status in the family. It does not account for why it is so intolerable for a narcissistic person's status to be anything but superior.

The pursuit and attainment of status defends against unbearable feelings of worthlessness that result when this motivation is frustrated (Afek, 2018; Kernberg, 1970; Kohut, 2009). These shadow feelings are dissociated from and life is structured to keep them at bay (Afek, 2018; Diamond & Meehan, 2013). This is why it is so important for the narcissist to attain their status objectives. The alternative is too painful to accept.

Avoiding the pain of not being highest status can render all other pursuits meaningless. This includes love (Kealy & Ogrodniczuk, 2014). There is no room in the pursuit of status for dependence on others (Kernberg, 2014). High-status people must only have others depend on them - if at all. Dependence leads to the unbearable shame of inferiority. The rub is that in order for someone else to matter they have to be depended on in some way. So nobody can matter enough to the narcissist to be loved. Kealy and Ogrodniczuk wisely postulate that this inability to love extends to the narcissist's self.

> *The times Chavon did not feel superior were agonizing for her. She was consumed in shame. She had no one to talk to about this because she knew they would just say it was her fault she did not attain superiority. And that would only make her feel worse. She had to do whatever it took to keep these feelings at bay.*

She played soccer and if she had a bad game she blamed her coach for putting her in the wrong position. If she did not get an A on a test, she would lie to her parents that she did. If she did not feel like she was the center of attention at school, she would make up an illness she was suffering from to solicit sympathy and attention.

What happens when the patchwork falls apart?

In two words: vindictive aggression. When others do not reflect back the narcissist's exaggerated self-importance they tend to lash out in retaliation (Kjærvik & Bushman, 2021; Kealy & Ogrodniczuk 2011). This aggression can take the form of a "hot" reaction or calculated effort to punish the person they feel wounded by. Anyone who stands in the way of a narcissist feeling superior can face their aggression.

Chavon fashioned herself as extremely intelligent, attractive, a leader, and a great athlete. She expected to be shown deference from others. Sometimes she would encounter someone who was not awed by her. They might interrupt her when she was talking or speak up about their own accomplishments. This enraged Chavon. She felt like this other person was taking away the attention and admiration that she was entitled to.

Chavon would find a way to get back at such people. Usually this amounted to disparaging them behind their backs to others. Over time, their reputation would be torn down and Chavon would resume her place of superiority.

How do they shore up their self-worth?

Their status-based exaggerated self-worth is as essential as it is fragile. As a result they must develop coping styles that reinforce their sense of superiority and negate threats to it. These styles involve exploiting others.

Kernberg argues that a narcissist cannot tolerate seeing others as separate from them (2014). It is too disruptive to their sense of dominance over others and threatens the helplessness they work so hard to avoid. As such, a narcissist may assume that others are extensions of themselves. They are to be used as needed by the narcissist - just as you would use your hand to grab what you need.

A narcissist uses others to protect their inflated self-worth by dividing their interpersonal world into allies and enemies (Back, 2013). Doing so, provides experiences of mutual admiration with their allies. It also relocates their dreaded feelings of worthlessness to their enemies. An enemy is anyone who challenges or undermines the narcissist's pursuit of status. An ally is someone who facilitates this pursuit either by showing admiration or possessing high status themselves showing affinity to the narcissist.

How do they relocate their worthlessness into enemies?

A narcissist can engage in a subtle yet powerful psychological maneuver to find the worthlessness they cannot stand in themselves in others - known as pathological projective identification (Ogden, 1979; Reid & Kealy, 2022).

Projective identification is thought to be a common – and often benign – occurrence when relational communication needs to happen without language. Imagine a dog who makes eye contact with his owner, then turns around and deliberately walks away while keep his eyes locked on them as if the owner is about to give chase. The owner finds himself in a sudden playful state and does give chase.

The process becomes pathological when there is an asymmetric relationship and the more powerful party uses the other party to rid themselves of unwanted feelings. This is what happens when a narcissist employs this maneuver. First, they identify the 'enemy' over whom they have some leverage. This can take the form of dependency (e.g. parent to a child) and/or authority (e.g. boss to a report). Next, the narcissist unconsciously registers the threat of feeling worthless and finds it unbearable. So, they unconsciously relocate - or project - these feelings into the less powerful party. The narcissist is now convinced that it is the other who is worthless. The job is not done, however. They need the other person to act the part to feel fully convinced that they are not the worthless one. So, a narcissist can deprive, devalue and control the other to influence that person to experience themselves as worthless. Now the job is done and the narcissist's feelings of worthlessness are safely confined in their 'enemy'.

An example best illustrates this.

> *In eleventh grade Chavon moved to a new school. She quickly ascertained the social pecking order in her class and buddied up to the high status students. There was another student in the class named Debbie who was decidedly not in the popular group. Chavon worried that she might become like Debbie if the cool kids got to know her better. So, she set about to keeping the focus on Debbie and off of her. She whispered in class to her friends about Debbie's 'gross clothes'. She would invite Debbie to sit with them at lunch then rebuke her when she approached their table. Chavon would mockingly laugh at Debbie for thinking she could sit with her.*
>
> *This trend of bullying led to Debbie feeling very bad about herself. Upon seeing the signs of this Chavon felt relieved.*

Chavon could not tolerate the fear and worthlessness she felt upon moving to a new school and not knowing if she would be liked. She used pathological projective identification to relocate these intolerable feelings into Debbie. Since Chavon had achieved a higher social status by getting in with the popular crowd, she had leverage over Debbie - who also wanted access to this group. Chavon alternately deprived and devalued Debbie into thinking and feeling like she was worthless. The relief Chavon felt once Debbie had identified as worthless came from feeling safe from these feelings - at Debbie's great expense.

A narcissist who employs pathological projective identification with another has to be right about their perceptions (Ogden, 1979). They may fear psychological extinction if they have to consciously claim this aspect of themselves. The narcissist may be convinced at a deep level that they would have nobody to safely express these feelings to so that they could feel more regulated and able to be soothed. Instead, the feelings must be ejected and found--communicated with absolute certainty--in the other. There is no set of verbal counterarguments that can convince the narcissist otherwise in such moments. As Ogden succinctly puts it, the narcissist's logic goes something like: "I can only see in you what I put there, and so if I don't see that in you, I see nothing" (1979, p. 360). In order to occupy a shared reality with a narcissist under these circumstances the other must go along. Refusal to comply could destroy the only form of connection that is available--something the other may have to avoid at all costs.

Do they feel bad for using others like this?

In short, no. First, they lack the kind of empathy needed to feel genuine concern for the feelings of others. Although they can cognitively grasp how others might feel they are not emotionally moved by this understanding (Weinberg & Ronningstam, 2022). They might notice how devaluing another could make the other feel inadequate but would not care. Since 'ruth' is defined as compassion for the misery of another, the narcissist's lack of empathy leaves them in a perpetual state of ruth*less*ness.

Second, a narcissist can be prone to deception. Research shows they report more unethical behavior - including lying - in day to day situations than others (Azizli et al., 2016; Baughman et al., 2014; Jonason et al., 2014). They place little value on honest communication - particularly if it interferes with their pursuit of status (Oliveira & Levine, 2008). If telling the truth does not benefit them, then they will not hesitate to distort it.

Chavon was unconcerned about the suffering she inflicted upon the Debbie's in her life. She just did not think of these others with any hint of remorse. She could feign concern for others when she thought it would give someone a good impression of her.

Chavon was not bound by any sort of moral principles. All that mattered was securing her sense of being better than others. If she de-prioritized this mission she would feel too bad for anything else to matter. So, she would wear a mask of charm and charisma. She was careful to only let certain people see her rageful and vindictive sides. These people had to be lower status so that she could refute their claims about her.

For example, Chavon one time saw Debbie after school. They were alone in a hallway. All of Chavon's displaced rage at the worthlessness she had transferred to Debbie came bubbling up. "What is your problem?," she accusingly asked Debbie.

Debbie, felt a surge of fear, no terror, go through her. "What?"

"You heard me!", Chavon spit out. "Nobody likes you and you don't seem to get it."

Debbie's head lowered and she did not answer. Chavon's rage was shifting to triumph.

The next day, Debbie told the one friend she still had in the popular clique, Stacey, about how Chavon had treated her. At the lunch table the next day, Stacey directly asked Chavon, "What did you say to Debbie yesterday?"

Chavon instantly realized that if her friends knew about the cruelty she showed Debbie that she could lose her status in the group. "Nothing, why?" she lied.

Stacey said, "Well she said that you told her nobody liked her. She was crying as she told me this."

Chavon feigned astonishment and said, "I have no idea what she's talking about. I saw her in the hallway and said hello. That's it. What is up with her? She's always *had something against me and I've been nothing but good to her."*

Chavon was pleased to see that her other friends were agreeing with her.

So, a child born to the person described here finds someone who:
- Is consistently pursuant of higher status for themselves.
- Intent on pairing with allies who can boost their status.
- Equally intent on devaluing enemies to boost their status.
- Is thin-skinned and easily wounded by challenges to their authority.
- Is incapable of loving themselves and others.
- Cannot genuinely feel nor value love others may have for them.
- Sees their own thoughts and feelings as most important so anyone who asserts their perspective is 'selfish'.
- Copes with a core sense of worthlessness by denial, projection onto another and getting that other to identify with this worthlessness.
- Lacks genuine concern for the feelings of others.
- Is capable and willing to deceive others for their own benefit.

When a child enters the world of a narcissistic parent

Parenthood poses a challenge for a narcissist. The child's developmental needs can threaten the parent with states of deprivation, devaluation and powerlessness.

Deprivation

Their child may compete for attention and admiration. Such competition may deprive the parent of the admiration they feel entitled to. This deprivation can threaten the narcissistic parent with their dreaded feelings of worthlessness.

Devaluation

If the child is gifted in a realm the narcissistic parent cares about then the parent can feel devalued. Through no fault of the child's own, the parent can experience envy towards that child. Envy is a feeling of inadequacy due to someone possessing something the parent does not. Next, comes a vindictive effort to destroy what that person has so the parent feels more adequate. If a child's natural gifts challenge the parent's sense of superiority then the child's mere existence can be cause for envy and vindictiveness in that parent.

Powerlessness

A narcissistic parent may be threatened with intolerable feelings of powerlessness when their child seeks autonomy. An infant is obviously helpless and vulnerable. The narcissistic parent may feel gratified by the child's dependence on them. As the infant grows and develops their own center of initiative they may come into conflict with the parent. Children at ages 1 to 3 seek a sense of independence from their parent (Erikson, 1968). This often means opposing the parent with the hope that doing so will not compromise the parent's love for the child. The child wants to assert their independence and know their parent can handle it. A narcissistic parent may see the child's healthy attempts to defy the parent's commands as efforts to make the parent powerless.

> *Chavon went to college and graduated with high honors. She found a boyfriend in her senior year who put her on a pedestal. He would never assert his preferences if they conflicted with hers. Chavon felt superior in the relationship and this helped her stay propped up internally. She was prone to throwing fits of rage if her boyfriend, named James, failed to meet any of her expectations.*
>
> *After college, James found a job in the same city as Chavon was moving to. Shortly after he proposed to her. She accepted. Chavon worked as a software engineer and excelled in her role. She made all of the decisions in*

her relationship. Weekends were predicated on what she wanted to do. If James asked for time to pursue something important to him she would accuse him of being 'selfish' and uncaring. He would invariably drop his request and seek her 'forgiveness' in such moments.

Chavon's unchecked superiority was jeopardized with the birth of her daughter - Samantha. Chavon initially saw parenthood as an opportunity to mold a child into her likeness. She confessed to James that she was excited to have a miniature version of herself running around the house. James did not demur. He was relieved that his wife seemed happy in the moment instead of upset with him.

Samantha did not fit Chavon's bill, however. She seemed to have an unending amount of needs that Chavon had to meet. From waking in the middle of night to breast feed to stopping her workday to change Samantha's diapers. Chavon quickly felt like Samantha was taking her place as the center of attention and felt deprived. She also felt devalued by the mandate to meet Samantha's needs ahead of her own. She made sense of this as Samantha's needs taking more importance than hers. Finally, she felt powerless as a mother to Samantha. When Samantha turned two she became willful and stopped obeying her mother's every command. Chavon's new inability to make Samantha obey her led to feeling intolerably powerless.

The narcissistic parent's solution: Scapegoat their child

In order for the narcissistic parent to escape feelings of deprivation, devaluation and powerlessness they segregate their family into allies and enemies. Allies are family members deemed to be superior along with the parent. Enemies are family members who prove the narcissistic parent's superiority by being inferior.

A narcissistic parent can put a child into the role of enemy. I will refer to the child in this role as the scapegoat. The term scapegoat comes from the Old Testament. In preparation for the Day of Atonement, or Yom Kippur, the Jewish people performed a ritual involving two goats. One of the goats was subject to sacrificial slaughter, while the members of the community pinned their sins upon the other. That second goat was then cast into exile in a rocky headland away from the village, taking the sins with it. It became known as the scapegoat.

By putting their child in the role of scapegoat the narcissistic parent restores their superior status. They do this by flipping the script on the ways the child may threaten their status. The narcissistic parent deprives this child of needed emotional nourishment. They also devalue the child in attitude and action. And they domineer the child. They ensure the child will not make decisions without worrying about the parent's reaction. These three tactics result in the scapegoat child embodying the deprivation, devaluation and powerlessness the narcissistic parent was initially threatened by. Now it is the narcissistic parent with the highest status in the family, followed by their 'allies', and the scapegoat child with the lowest.

> Chavon's narcissistic defenses kicked into high gear to deal with the threats posed by her daughter. She insisted on getting a full-time nanny so she did not have to spend as much time with Samantha. She began to deprive Samantha of the kind of emotional nourishment all kids need. She thought to herself, "This kid is so needy and selfish. She needs to learn that not everything is about her." Under this rationale, she would respond to Samantha's requests for her mother's attention with eyerolls and exasperation. She would tell Samantha not to interrupt her when she is busy and to stop thinking the world revolves around her.
>
> Chavon began to see Samantha as defective. She saw an unruly, rude, and self-centered child in her daughter and treated her accordingly. She would complain to her husband about how Samantha misbehaved in one way or another. James would join in on reprimanding Samantha to show he was staunchly on Chavon's side. Chavon's lack of love for her daughter was not a fault of her own. It reflected how difficult Samantha was to love.
>
> As Chavon shifted the deprivation and devaluation onto Samantha she began to feel better. Her old sense of being superior was starting to come back. So long as she could keep putting Samantha down in these ways Chavon could feel superior.

Then came a wrinkle. Samantha started pre-school and was well liked by her teacher and classmates. Many of her friends asked their parents to have Samantha over for play dates. On these occasions Samantha felt wanted. She would come home with a sense of pride in who she was. She would be less willing to submit to her mother's deprivation and devaluation. She complained at her mother's refusal to pay attention to her. She argued back when her mother accused her of being rude and selfish. This infuriated Chavon.

She realized that Samantha's participation in relationships outside the family brought her happiness and this led to being less willing to be her mother's scapegoat. Chavon solved this by severing Samantha's relationships outside the family. She needed Samantha to be isolated from everyone but her. Only then could Chavon control Samantha in the way she needed to. So, she refused invitations for play dates and would scold Samantha for complaining about not being able to see her friends. Over time, Samantha gave up trying to have friendships outside the family.

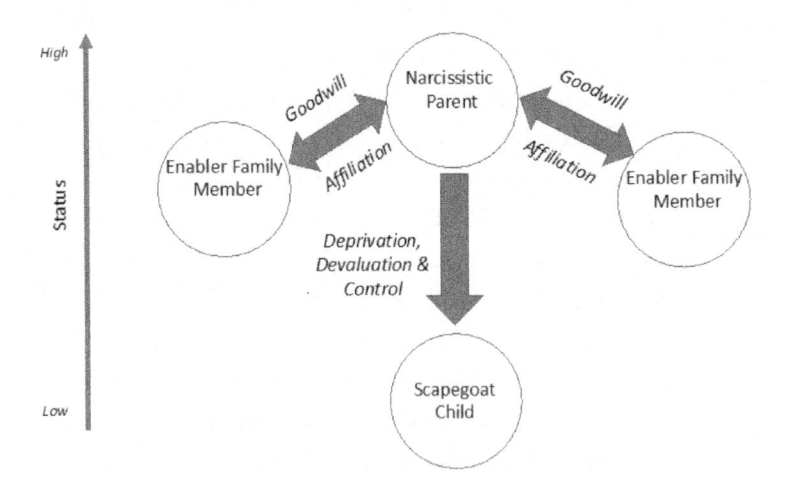

Figure 1.1 How the narcissistically abusive parent and family treats the scapegoat child

Impacts on the scapegoat child

Now that we understand the world the scapegoat child to a narcissistic parent enters, we can explore the impacts on the child. The child's experience is marked by this core conflict: if they seek the status they are developmentally entitled to they jeopardize their place in their parent's reality. The following chapters will address the adaptations the child is forced to make to survive.

3

The Scapegoat Child's Role & Symptoms in Narcissistic Abuse

> *Did your parent look at you with suspicion?*
> *Was it a matter of when - not if - they put you down?*
> *Did you grow up assuming you were just a 'bad' kid?*

If you grew up with a narcissistic parent and felt devalued, deprived and controlled most of the time then you were that parent's scapegoat. The scapegoat is someone who must embody what the narcissistic parent cannot stand in themselves. By "finding" what they hate in themselves to be in the scapegoat child, the parent feels protected. This is the *role* of the scapegoat child.

The scapegoat child has to maneuver themselves to participate in their parent's world. These maneuvers are necessary to manage the terrifying awareness that their parent is hostile towards the child's growth, joy, and authentic self. Aligning with the narcissistic parent's devaluation, deprivation, and control of them can make this situation survivable. The ways a child does this are the *symptoms* of the scapegoat child.

How the scapegoat role develops

A narcissistic parent is in a constant battle to keep their self-hatred at bay. They deny such feelings and insist on their opposite. Instead of experiencing themselves as worth less than others they are worth more. They relocate their bad feelings into the scapegoat child and exaggerate their own good feelings. This results in devaluing that child while requiring admiration and obedience in return.

A scapegoat child's growth threatens the narcissistic parent's fragile and inflated self-worth. Growth is a vitalizing and self-enhancing experience. Such experiences conflict with the child seeming less than the narcissistic parent.

The scapegoat child's growth puts them at odds with the narcissistic parent. If the child revels in their developmental achievements they will be met with more hostility. If they disown their expanding abilities they may be spared. Only the latter strategy feels survivable to the child.

A scapegoat child can disown their own growth by believing they are defective and dangerous. In the first case the child doubts their ability to grow. They see themselves as dispossessed of their own expanding capabilities. They believe that they cannot do anything right.

A scapegoat child who believes their growth is dangerous will also disavow it. Their increased physical strength could make them hurt other people. Their developing sexual identity is sinister and shameful. Their increased perceptiveness hurts others' feelings.

The scapegoat child's role requires them to sacrifice their growth to remain less than the narcissistic parent. The child has to collude with the parent's claim that the problem in their relationship is the child's growth. The child has no recourse to the real issue: that the narcissistic parent cannot tolerate the child's development.

Now the parent seems less cruel when they are hostile towards the scapegoat child's displays of growth. A child who believes their growth is defective or dangerous can see their parent's hostility as justified. The parent is no longer wrong for treating the child with contempt.

Functions of the scapegoat child's role

Once the child accepts the scapegoat role, they can attach to a rejecting parent. The child faces rejection because they are accused of being what the narcissistic parent rejects in themselves. The narcissistic parent will refuse to know this child in any other way. Now, the child stomachs their feelings of hurt and anger at the parent's cruelty. They *deserve* such treatment, after all.

Assuming the scapegoat role also lets the child perceive the narcissistic parent as good and helpful to them. These are necessary perceptions to survive as a small child. The child has to live in a world with a parent who is only trying to help them be better.

How the child participates as the scapegoat

Everything I have explained so far is at a conceptual level. In practice, this happens with powerful subtlety for the child and the narcissistic parent. It is in interactions with the parent when the child can suddenly find themselves to deserve the parent's abuse.

The child is aware that the hostile parent 'knows' there is something fundamentally wrong with the child. Being treated this way by a narcissistic parent can feel like an invasion of the child's mind. Like being possessed. The child's feeling of being deeply defective is intrusive, disturbing, smothering, and inescapable in these moments.

In contrast, the narcissistic parent finds themselves and is seen by the child to be flawless. This is because the scapegoat child is the only one who can have flaws. It must be this way for the narcissistic parent to emotionally stay afloat.

> *Isaiah had been in therapy for several years. He came to treatment because he could not shake a sense of feeling deeply inadequate. He felt this way no matter how he was received in his work, friendships, or relationships. All tended to be positive for him. He was well aware that his narcissistic mother had forced him into the scapegoat role. Now he and I were identifying how this role showed up when he got close to people today.*
>
> *In one session, Isaiah talked about being happy that he would be promptly reimbursed by his insurance for the*

sessions. He said, "I can't believe the insurance company is being an efficient provider for me."

This term struck me, and I asked, "What about inefficient providers? Are you familiar with that?"

Immediately, Isaiah was convinced that I was pointing toward his psychopathology. He thought, "He must be referring to how I don't give people enough of a chance. That if they don't provide for all of my needs perfectly I drop them. He thinks I am narcissistic. And I must be!"

Isaiah felt guilty of these internal accusations. He felt lower than me, and a searing shame came over him. He could not say or do anything to prove his innocence, but maybe he could get his sentence reduced. So Isaiah tried to cut me off at the pass and preemptively see himself as defective.

He said, "Well, yeah, I guess I have often cut people out when they don't meet my needs. I guess I'm too sensitive about that stuff."

But then he stopped. His mind settled a bit. He felt some trust towards me that had developed over the year we had been working together. "Wait a minute, why did you ask me that question?" he asked me.

I said, "Well, when you said efficient provision, I was struck by it. I thought it might open something *important up. I wasn't sure what, but I went where my instinct took me."*

Isaiah exclaimed, "Wow! I just realized that I heard your question as an indictment of my psychology. That you had found what was wrong with me, and you were leading me to see what it was. I thought you were laying bare how I am really the narcissistic one who can't stand imperfections in others."

Even as Isaiah talked about it, he still felt like he was in the situation. "It feels like something permanent. Like there's nothing to be done to fix or repair this sense that you found something wrong with me."

Isaiah's experience with me shows how quickly the ways of participating in a narcissistic relationship can show up. Just like in earlier situations with his narcissistic mother, he had to be the one who was wrong. In this case, he had enough trust in his therapist and distance from his narcissistic abuser that he could question it all. He asked me what I meant by the question. My answer shed light to both of them on how fast and consuming the scapegoat role struck Isaiah.

Maneuvers like the one Isaiah made in this session are born out of having to attach to a hostile, narcissistic parent. Assuming the role of scapegoat allowed Isaiah to have a reality that was shared with his mother. He suffered tremendously, but it was better than having no shared reality with anyone at the time.

The scapegoat child's symptoms

The symptoms of the scapegoat child are the ways the child must treat themselves to comply with the scapegoat role. This can mean constructing an inner critic that is hellishly harsh. The child can feel like everything they do is embarrassing, stupid and/or wrong. It may be quite different on the outside, but this is what goes on inside the child.

The symptoms of anxiety are prominent. The scapegoat child feels an anxious inevitability that someone else will discover their defect.

Unkind relationships can be another symptom. Since the scapegoat child's mind is so primed to be found as defective, the child might find friends who treat them poorly too. They may seek the only reality they know in their family outside of their family too.

By design, the scapegoat child is not allowed to feel self-esteem. Feeling proud of oneself would have prevented them from being the scapegoat to the narcissistic parent. Life without the possibility of self-worth is a dreary proposition. The consequence of this is a symptom of chronic depression marked by hopelessness.

4

Two Ways a Scapegoat Survivor Keeps Their Narcissistic Parent Around

> *Is it still hard to be kind to yourself despite 'knowing' you are not as bad as you were told you were as a child?*
> *Do you still feel blocked or scared when you try to do what you are good at?*
> *Do you wonder why it's so hard to feel safe in the world even though you are no longer in immediate danger?*

Adult scapegoat survivors of a narcissistic parent can find it very hard to see and treat themselves positively. "How can childhood experiences still impact me today?" they may wonder. They may even conclude: "There must be something wrong with me that I can't just 'get over it'."

If this experience resonates with you, it is important to understand why the effects of being a scapegoat child last into adulthood. But the reason will not just be because things were really bad back then. There are two ways adult scapegoat survivors carry their relationship with their narcissistic parent into the present.

Our early worlds are shaped by the people in it - for better or worse[2]

The people who make up the child's world determine the emotional contours and possibilities the child can experience. No one has a greater influence than the child's parents.

As a very small person in a very big world, a child needs a big person to depend on for food, protection, and love. The child's physical and emotional needs can initially only be met by their parent. So, the young child is incentivized by survival to stay close to that parent.

The parent's responses will largely determine what the child's life feels like. If the child's parent is responsive and available to them, then their world will seem friendly and providing. And if the child's parent is unresponsive and frightening, then their world will seem uncaring and dangerous.

A child cannot swap out the world they are in if they do not like it. Evolution says they must stay close to their parent to have the highest odds of survival. The child has to do this regardless of the

---

[2] This chapter is based upon the theory and research of Lorna Smith Benjamin. The concepts I describe are laid out in greater detail in her book:

Benjamin, L. S. (2006). Interpersonal reconstructive therapy: An integrative, personality-based treatment for complex cases. Guilford Press.

quality of relationship the parent offers them. They are programmed to see their parent as the only one who can supply what they need.

Meanwhile, the child is developing an internal map of who they are in relation to their internalized parent. Next, the child populates their internal map with the behaviors, thoughts, and feelings that bring the child closer to their internalized parent. When the child engages in these actions, thinks these thoughts and feels these feelings they are close to their internalized parent. When the child acts, thinks or feels otherwise they are more distant from the internal parent. The child pursues closeness to the internal parent, whether that makes the child feel good or bad. Closeness means being somebody to someone. Distance risks being nobody to no one.

When closeness to a parent means suffering

In a good-enough upbringing, the child generally feels close to their parent. That closeness is not contingent on the child meeting the parent's needs. The parent is content to see their child explore and return for nurturance as needed. This kind of stance tells the child that their parent is there for them when they need them.

A child with this kind of history will have an easy time relating to their internalized parent. They feel close to their internalized parent when they do what makes themselves happy. Their internalized parent wants what is good for them.

Scapegoat children of narcissistic parents have to manufacture a feeling of closeness. The child has no consistent experience of feeling safe with and cared for by this parent. They have been used to embody the worthlessness that the narcissistic parent feels in themselves yet cannot tolerate.

So, being close to their internalized narcissistic parent hurts. The child's internalized parent endorses the child feeling shame and despair, thinking they are undeserving and defective, and taking self-sabotaging actions. When the child engages in these experiences, they feel closer to their internalized parent.

Two ways a scapegoat child stays close to their internalized narcissistic parent

The scapegoat child and later adult survivor stays close to their internalized narcissistic parent by either treating themselves the way their parent treated them or living as if the narcissistic parent is still around and in charge.

Treating yourself the way your narcissistic parent treated you

Many scapegoat survivors live with intense self-criticism. Their narcissistic parent may have criticized and berated them to make them feel worthless. Self-criticism is a way of treating themselves the way their narcissistic parent treated them. There is often a hard-to-define quality that makes the scapegoat survivor feel like they are doing what they are supposed to be doing when they attack themselves like this. That quality is the closeness to the internalized narcissistic parent that self-criticism creates.

> Mike grew up with a narcissistic father who regularly attacked him. His "offenses" amounted to not being able to read his father's mind and do his bidding. When his father came home from work in the evenings, it was a matter of when not if he started yelling at Mike. Typically the offense was around not doing something his father had asked him to do. Mike would have to sit through his father's tirade about how "selfish," "irresponsible," "inconsiderate," and "immature" Mike was.
>
> Mike's father also had qualities that Mike admired. His father could be funny when he wanted to be. He was charismatic to people outside the family. And he always "seemed" to know what to say or do. Mike's mother did not have much of a presence in Mike's life. She was quiet and avoided conflict. She would not protect Mike from his father's abuse.
>
> Away from his father Mike found himself intensely criticizing himself. If he was walking down the hallway in high school and said hello to a peer he would hear his own voice and find it weak and embarrassing. Then he would feel disgust towards himself for saying hello in such an awkward way. He would be filled with anger at himself and shame. There was little to nothing Mike could do to reassure himself in such instances. The fact that the other person did not seem to find anything

wrong with Mike's greeting did not matter. Just as Mike's father's tirades towards him felt inevitable so was Mike's criticism of himself.

Mike would often wonder at his private self-condemnation in these moments. It seemed so at odds with how people outside of his family received him in his life. He was generally well-liked and respected by these people. Nonetheless, what felt more authentic to him were the excoriating attacks he would launch at himself.

These attacks were how Mike stayed close to his internalized narcissistic father. Given the lack of viable alternatives in his family he had to find a way to do this. His father was the only game in town and Mike had to find a way to play in it. Self-criticism did the trick.

Since self-criticism can result in feeling closer to one's internalized narcissistic parent it can be very hard to break this practice. It is not something you can argue yourself out of. Instead the survivor needs to find and cultivate new relationships as viable alternatives to the internalized parent.

Living as if your narcissistic parent is still around and in charge

There is another subtle but powerful way a scapegoat survivor can stay close to their internalized narcissistic parent. When the survivor complies with the belief that they are defective and/or undeserving they are living as though their narcissistic parent is still around and in charge. As painful as this feels for the survivor it creates a sense of closeness to the internalized parent.

When a scapegoat child shies away from their own strength they are keeping close to the narcissistic parent in this manner. The world that the narcissistic parent was in charge of forbade the scapegoat child from knowing their own strength. Thwarting your own capabilities is a way of keeping the narcissistic parent in charge today.

I want to emphasize that the scapegoat survivor does not consciously choose to keep the narcissistic parent around in this way. Rather they are governed by the unconscious demand to stay close to their internalized narcissistic parent. Failing to do this could result in being nobody to no one. Until there is a viable alternative, survival requires the survivor to maintain this closeness. And acting as though the parent is still around and in charge is a means to this end.

> *Noah grew up with a domineering and vindictive narcissistic mother. She thwarted his attempts to be his own person throughout childhood and adolescence. If he was more than one minute late coming home from a social engagement she would scream at him about his "disrespect for the household rules". He was on restriction or grounded more often than not throughout high school. Over time he stopped forging friendships outside his home. He was too weary of the unwinnable*

battles he had to fight with her to be able to have a social life. His parents had divorced long ago so Noah had no adult to intervene on his behalf. He developed painful ideas that he was defective and unlikeable to others. These beliefs deterred him from seeking connection outside his home thereby sparing him further conflict with his mother.

After college, Noah took a job at a consulting firm downtown. He initially found the role to be interesting and meaningful in its purpose. Around the same time he started therapy because he felt like his life just was not working. He always felt under pressure to accomplish his goals and this created intense anxiety most of the time. I asked him about his upbringing and Noah spoke about how his mother treated him for the first time in his life. I reacted with astonishment at what Noah described and emphasized how she undeservedly abused him. Initially he felt relieved to know that he was not as bad as she claimed. As the therapy wore on and he began to share all the ways he was mistreated the rest of his life started to suffer. He found it much harder to focus at work. This led to delays in his ability to meet deadlines and reprimands from his supervisors. He retreated from his friends because he did not feel like he could be honest with them about what he was going through. He stopped doing things that were healthy like exercising and eating healthy food.

I understood this digression in his life as a way of unconsciously staying close to his internalized narcissistic mother. By thwarting his professional and social success he was acting as if she was still around and in charge. The players were different but the script played out very similarly to his high school years. It took some time in therapy before Noah could find the therapeutic relationship to be a viable alternative to his internalized mother. My steadfast empathic support of him seemed critical in this respect.

The 3 Pillars of Recovery can help you live as though you are the one who is now in charge. These three principles help scapegoat survivors understand how they are staying close to their internalized parent, structure their lives in ways that do not reinforce this closeness and find alternative relationships that let the survivor feel connected while living as though they are now in charge. Just as it is difficult to stop the practice of self-criticism if it creates closeness to the narcissistic parent so it is with living as though the parent is in charge. Viable relational alternatives to that parent are needed before one can surrender this practice. The scapegoat survivor needs convincing that they will still be somebody to someone else.

Pillar #1:

Making Sense of What Happened (So You Know It Was Not Your Fault)

5

Making Sense of What Happened with the First Pillar of Recovery

> *Do you have the nagging feeling that nothing you do in life is correct?*
> *Do you find it hard to experience yourself as good but all too easy to see it in others?*
> *Are you used to relationships and friendships where you give way more than you get yet still worry about being called 'selfish'?*

The first pillar of recovery helps you build a new frame of reference for what you experienced as a scapegoat child to a narcissistic parent. You get to question whether you deserved such abuse or not. You become able to see your parent's problems not just the problems you were told you have.

The scapegoat child must accept their parent's abuse

In his 2005 commencement address to Kenyon College, author David Foster Wallace told the parable of the old fish swimming by two young fish and asking them, 'How's the water?' After the young fish swim by, one turns to the other and asks, 'What's water?' (Wallace, 2009).

The scapegoat child's water involved devaluation, deprivation and control. The only way for the child to make sense of these cruelties was to assume they deserved them. Doing so allowed them to establish and maintain a bind to their narcissistic parent. I use the term 'bind' instead of 'bond' purposely. A bind *forces* two people to stick together. A bond is a mutually close relationship *that results* from closeness to each other.

The scapegoat child binds to their narcissistic parent and concludes that this is how things have to be. Just as the fish swims unquestioningly in water, so the scapegoat child believes they deserve the parent's mistreatment. Believing you deserve to be mistreated leaves you with no basis to challenge your parent's place in your mind. They are simply treating you the way everyone would treat you if they knew how wretched you are. The scapegoat child has no other frame of reference from which to realize they do not deserve this abuse.

The narcissistic parent has a privileged status in the scapegoat child's mind

There are two reasons the scapegoat child cannot question how their narcissistic parent treats them. The first reason has to do with isolation. The scapegoat child by definition does not have allies in the family. As such, they have no one to talk with about what is happening and make sense of it in a way where they are not to blame. Attempts to talk to other enabling family members can result in the child feeling even more alienated. They may be told to 'stop complaining' or that their narcissistic parent 'really loves' them.

The second reason the child cannot question the narcissistic parent has to do with their cognitive abilities. Up until around the age of five years old, children tend to think egocentrically. This means that when good things happen it is because they deserve them. And when bad things happen it is also because they deserve them. The young child trying to make sense of how their narcissistic parent is devaluing them has to assume this is happening because they deserve it. The child has not yet developed the cognitive ability to take the other's perspective. As a result they cannot attribute their parent's mistreatment of them to something about that parent. This would be required for the child to question the narcissistic parent's status in their mind.

All of this results in the scapegoat child giving the narcissistic parent a privileged position in the their mind. The parent holds the most authority out of the two of them. The child must orient their feelings, thoughts, and decisions around the parent.

The narcissistic parent's ongoing influence in the scapegoat survivor's life

The scapegoat survivor carries the narcissistic parent with them by living as though the narcissistic parent is around and in charge or by treating oneself as the parent did. In this diagram, you can see how it is necessary for the scapegoat child to stay close to the internalized narcissistic parent.

Being Close to an Internalized Narcissistic Parent

Nobody to No One

Nobody to No One

The Scapegoat Child Gets to Be a Bad Somebody to a Superior Someone

The child finds a way to stay bound to the narcissistic parent by identifying with the parent's cast-off worthlessness. This protects them from losing their parent's willingness to stay connected to them. By extension the child is protected from being nobody to no one. The tradeoff is that the scapegoat child has to be a <u>bad somebody to a superior someone</u>.

When Susan was being raised by her parents she did not think there was anything different about her family. She struggled with intense social anxiety at school despite being well-liked. In her mind, she would go over interactions she had with her friends and skewer herself for saying or doing 'the wrong thing'.

At home she knew to be very careful with what she said around her parents. Her father could start yelling at her at the drop of a hat. Her mother seemed to watch Susan and report any supposed 'wrongdoing' to her father. Susan never felt safe in her home and did not think she should. She assumed that her parents were only hostile towards her because she was such a bad kid.

It was not until she found herself in therapy in her late twenties that she learned she had been mistreated. Susan was telling me about her worries that she will say or do the wrong thing around people.

I asked, "Do you recall feeling this way when you were young? Like around other family members?"

Susan immediately said, "Well, yeah! I mean I was always getting in trouble for speaking disrespectfully to my Dad."

"Really? What sort of disrespectful things would you say?" I asked.

"Well, it was more like my tone of voice. He would tell me that I was speaking to him in a snide and disrespectful tone."

Susan went on to give example after example of the molehills that her father made into mountains as justification for his devaluation of her.

I eventually said, "Susan, it sounds like your father had inflated expectations of what he deserved. It also sounds like he hurt you if you did not meet these inflated expectations. And further it seems like he and your mother treated you as if you were the reason for all of the family's problems. And none of this seems to be an accurate reflection of who you are based on my experience with you."

Susan was blown away. It was so strange to think that things were not what they seemed in her upbringing. This was the first step in what was to be a long but important journey.

How Pillar #1 helps scapegoat survivors build a new frame of reference

The first pillar of recovery is to make sense of what happened in the narcissistic abuse to realize it was not your fault. This pillar involves learning about pathological narcissism and its effects on others. It may take the form of watching YouTube videos, reading books, blogs, and/or academic papers. There are two features to this pillar:

1) Redefining the problem

The scapegoat child had to see themselves as the main problem in their lives. They were too needy, lazy, unlikeable etc. to deserve their narcissistic parent's love. Or they were not enough of some trait to deserve that love.

As the scapegoat survivor absorbs information about pathological narcissists they learn how common it is for their children to feel like they are the problem. The scapegoat survivor learns how the narcissistic parent relocates their own sense of worthlessness into the scapegoat child. They begin to make sense of their lifelong feelings of defectiveness as a result of their parent's psychological problem rather than their own.

As a result of redefining the problem, the scapegoat survivor begins to question their narcissistic parent's privileged status in their mind. The scapegoat child has been required to see the parent as superior to themselves. Their parent would not recognize them as anything but inferior. If the child did not do this then they risked being nobody to no one. The information learned in this step makes it much more difficult to see the parent as superior. The survivor grows to see the parent's insistence on their superiority as a product of pathological narcissism.

2) Consider new understandings of then and now

As the scapegoat survivor questions the narcissistic parent's superiority, new understanding becomes available. Many scapegoat survivors see themselves as being in need of redemption. When they look back at themselves, all they can see is the supposed error of their ways. This perception makes it very difficult to respect and like who they were in their past. The scapegoat survivor who makes sense of what happened gets to question this understanding.

Such realizations cultivate compassion towards yourself. You may feel less shame when you think of yourself and your past. Instead, you grow more curious about the forces that you had to contend with at the time. Now you include how your past choices and actions were responses to your parent's psychological problems. You see how they let you survive a situation that was stacked against you. You get to be on your own side as you reflect on yourself.

Thinking *about* the internalized narcissistic parent

This pillar helps you begin to notice the water you are swimming in. You go from seeing the world through the lens of having deserved your parent's devaluation, deprivation and control to *thinking about* this lens itself.

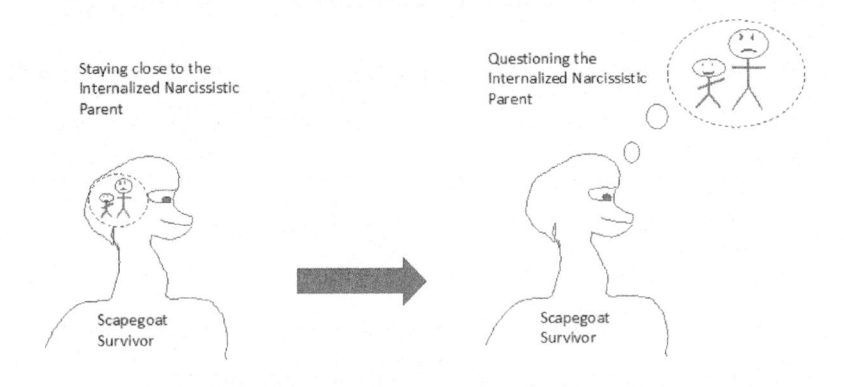

As you can see in this picture, the transition from acting from to thinking about creates space between you and the internalized narcissistic parent. It is a powerful shift that lets you claim more of your real self from your narcissistic parent's distortions about you.

6

Be The Scapegoat or Be Nobody To No One

> *Is it much easier to think about what's wrong with you than what's right with you?*
> *As painful as self-criticism is, does it seem like a necessary condition of existence?*
> *Is there an invisible barrier to feeling good in your life?*

Scapegoat survivors find it hard to think good thoughts about themselves. The scapegoat child to a narcissistic parent has to accept the ways the parent insists on interacting with them. This means the child feels inferior while the parent seems superior.

Why does the child go along with this? At a deep level the parent is utterly unwilling to see the child in a positive way. So, if the child shows that they feel good about who they are, they risk going unseen by their parent. Being psychologically invisible to a parent is far worse than being seen in a negative light. The best way to describe this experience is being nobody to no one. The child manages this threat by adapting to the role of scapegoat.

These necessary adaptations leave the scapegoat survivor unable to think positively about themselves. Scapegoat survivors may even grow frustrated with themselves for not being able to just 'snap out of it'. This chapter will help you develop compassion for yourself by appreciating the severity of what you had to overcome.

The child's need to find themselves in their parent's mind

Infants and young children are in the business of figuring out who they are in the world. Their biology and culture tells them to look to their parents as a reflection of themselves. Well-adjusted parents offer their child accurate and appreciative reflections of who that child is. These parents will not require the child to meet their own emotional needs. They will have enough emotional wherewithal in themselves to prioritize the child's needs.

In these arrangements the child is free to be themselves and expect to receive care as they are. A parent ensures this by showing that they are curious about, want to understand and appreciate the child's inner experience. There is no conflict for the child between being who they really are and how their parents see them. This allows the child to form a cohesive identity. They get to trust that how they experience themselves is very close to how others experience them. These children get to be somebody to someone without having to distort themselves.

The conditions of being found in the narcissistic parent's mind

The child of a narcissistic parent does face a conflict. The parent's denied sense of worthlessness takes priority in their psychology. They typically manage these feelings by insisting on their opposite. They consciously believe they are worth more than others. It is a tall order for them to stay convinced of this claim. So, they must continually contrast themselves with people they perceive as inferior. The child forced into the role of scapegoat is coerced to identify as inferior so the parent gets to be superior.

The narcissistic parent has a lot of tools to make the child go along with this. First, the parent feels entitled to be treated as superior. So the child's failure to revere the parent will be met with severe abuse. Second, the narcissistic personality does not have genuine empathy for others' feelings. So the child's appeals to be treated better will be of no consequence to the parent.

The parent's biggest advantage is the child's need to be known by the parent. When a narcissistic parent is intent on seeing the child as defective and undeserving, then the child's only choice is to be this. Why? The narcissistic parent is laying out the conditions under which they agree to know who the child is. These conditions are distorting and contemptible, but they are better than the alternative of becoming nobody to no one.

Camilla was in therapy in her late twenties because she felt extreme anxiety when she found success in her life. In the early sessions, she explained how she always had to watch out for her father growing up. He seemed to have it out for Camilla and would never pass up a chance to find fault with her decisions. She explained how whenever she tried to share her opinion with family members, they would roll their eyes and treat her like she did not know what she was talking about. Her father could only know her as a stupid person who did not know how to do anything right.

He was a history teacher at their local middle school. He fashioned himself as a scholar but never produced scholarly work. He liked to cite facts as a testament to his superior knowledge but lacked the ability to think critically and immersively about historical topics. He received average marks on his performance evaluations. He could not bear the feeling of being mediocre at his job. He would often complain about how his principal did not appreciate his gifts. Camilla noted that when he was criticizing her, his spirits seemed to perk up.

Camilla was intelligent, curious, and diligent. She especially excelled in writing critical essays on books assigned in her English class. She recalled two feelings when she had such assignments. First, she felt capable of finding an original point of view and writing about it. Second, she felt this undefinable nervousness. Like if she did this, some fabric of her universe might tear. She would put off these assignments until the night before they were due. Then she would work all night under the threat of not having anything to turn in. Once it was done, she did not feel proud of what she wrote, just relief that it was finished.

In therapy we understood how this painful writing process reflected the dilemma she faced. The only way she could be someone to somebody in her family was if she was ineffectual. She was an inherently effective thinker and writer. If she displayed her talents then she would be someone her father could not recognize. The nervousness she felt at having to do something she was good at reflected this conflict. These feelings were signaling to her that she was entering dangerous psychological territory. Beyond this rope was the agony of being nobody to no one.

The same warning system would go off when Camilla approached success at her job today. She was an assistant editor at a publishing company. After successfully editing her first book and receiving praise from her manager, she grew nervous. She began to doubt her abilities, saw this success as a fluke, and had difficulty concentrating on editing her next assignment. She felt frustrated with herself for not being able to perform like she did with the first book. In therapy we worked on developing a sense of compassion for herself in this process. That she was seeking to protect herself from the gravest of all dangers - being nobody to no one. She grew to accept that it would take time and empathy towards herself to fully know she could be her good, capable self and be somebody to someone.

The threat of being nobody to no one

The scapegoat child - and all children - exist so long as they feel like they are someone to their parent. When a narcissistic parent insists on their scapegoat child being worthless then this is the only way for this child to exist. For that child to know themselves as capable would jeopardize their psychological existence.

Being nobody to no one is to not exist. But it's worse than that because the sufferer continues existing in a certain sense. They do not feel real. They do not experience their parent as real and yet they remain conscious and breathing. Words do not do justice to how agonizing and endless such experiences can seem.

When the scapegoat child touches this experience, it is traumatizing. They must avoid it at all costs. Anxieties are created to warn the child of approaching this experience again. With a narcissistic parent, these anxieties will go off when the child begins to feel good about themselves. It is far better for the child to feel bad about themselves when feeling good means more trauma of this kind.

Coping with this threat today

Scapegoat survivors who faced the threat of being nobody to no one if they lived from the center of themselves may still expect that consequence for doing the same today. And, in a post-traumatic way, they may feel that this happens. For example, a creative scapegoat child who loved to paint would get great feedback from their first-grade teacher for doing so. The child felt special and capable. This experience conflicted with their father's attitude towards them that they could do nothing right. Over time, the prospect of painting felt dreadful. The child could not know at the time but they were up against the threat of becoming nobody to no one if they proceeded with what they were good at. In adulthood, this scapegoat survivor would experience severe dread and anxiety if they tried to paint. They could not focus and would have to stop after a short amount of time. It pained them that they could not safely do what they knew they wanted to do in their innermost being.

If this kind of experience resonates with you, there is hope. As you apply the three pillars of recovery in your life, the danger of being nobody to no one gradually diminishes. This is particularly true because of the new safe relationships you build. In the course of these relationships you get to have the actual experience that being all of who you are is welcome and appreciated. You get to stay somebody to someone when you are doing well – not just when you are flailing as it had to be with your narcissistic parent.

7

Neither the Scapegoat nor Golden Child Wins in Narcissistic Abuse

> *Were there clear favorites in your family?*
> *Did your parent prefer your sibling over you?*
> *Did your parent seem to prefer one child over the other?*

Different people may answer yes to the first two questions. This speaks to the different experiences children can have of the same narcissistic parent. If you were largely blamed, then your parents' diminishment of you likely made them feel better. And if you were largely exulted, then your parents' insistence on your perfection also made them feel better.

A family led by a narcissistic parent must revolve around that parent to survive. This means that different members will meet the different needs of that parent.

The scapegoat child helps the narcissistic parent deny their own sense of worthlessness. The golden child helps the narcissistic parent believe they are worth *more* than others. The parent may psychologically merge with this child. In such a merger, the child does not get to have their own opinions, needs, and fallibility. The narcissistic parent insists on their mutual perfection or else. The 'or else' is the knowledge that the parent would psychologically disown this child if they let the parent down. This means the child must live up to an impossibly high standard for the parent's sake - not their own.

Each child suffers. Neither role allows the child to be who they are. A narcissistic parent may use these roles to alienate siblings from each other. Sometimes the scapegoat child and the golden child have ways to reconcile. In other cases, they must put distance between themselves to avoid perpetuating the abuse their parent set in motion.

Why a narcissistic parent creates the scapegoat & golden child

Someone who is pathologically narcissistic lives in a binary world. They are either perfect or hopelessly defective. This can create an inner urgency to convince themselves they are perfect. Otherwise, they risk falling into the abyss of being abjectly inadequate. Shame, despair, hopelessness, and extreme self-hatred can ensue.

The narcissistic parent's internal arrangement leads to imposing roles upon the children. The parent can deny their fallibility - and the worthlessness it threatens - by scapegoating a child. The scapegoat child meets the parent's need to deny their imperfection.

The parent can then insist upon their perfection by fusing with the golden child. This child can do no wrong, according to the parent. Everything this child does reflects well on the parent. That is the unstated contract in this arrangement. Nothing the golden child achieves, however, is for themselves.

> Sharon was a pathologically narcissistic mother to her two children. Matt, her firstborn, became the scapegoat, and Marcia, his three-year younger sister, was the golden child.
>
> Sharon tried to center herself in all her relationships. She could not experience a sense of 'we' only 'me'.
>
> She married a man who characteristically put others' needs ahead of his own. She insisted on making all household decisions and took great offense if her husband ever objected. He learned to keep quiet.
>
> Sharon saw men as inferior and untrustworthy. Once her son was four years old, she began to see him in this light, too. He was developing his own will and mind, which made him less compliant. She worried that she would not be able to make him bend to her will, so she worked to make him feel like there was something wrong with him. If he doubted himself, he would be less likely to disobey her.
>
> At the same time, Sharon turned towards Marcia and showered her with praise and attention. She contrasted

Matt's supposed 'bad behavior' with Marcia's 'agreeableness'.

The costs to the children in these roles

Both the golden and scapegoat child are used by the narcissistic parent. On the surface it may look like one child is being treated poorly and the other is not. But neither child is being loved the way they deserve to be.

The scapegoat child has to adapt to an artificially bad identity. Whatever they do, think or feel gets construed as defective by the narcissistic parent. They are treated like an adversary to their parent. Meanwhile, it is their parent who is adversarial to them.

The golden child has to adapt to an artificially good identity. Whatever they do, think or feel gets construed as wonderful by the narcissistic parent. They are treated like a sparkling adjunct to their parent.

Neither child has a chance to develop their own identity in a realistic way. They are either being unrealistically diminished or exulted. They do not have a parent who can even-handedly reflect back to them who they are in the world. The parent is in too much of a rush to use each child for their own purposes.

Here are three costs that both children suffer:

Lack of agency

Neither child is expected nor allowed to be separate from the narcissistic parent. When children in either role make decisions that do not conform to their role, they face punishment. The scapegoat child who expresses pride will be diminished to keep them feeling worthless. The golden child who doubts their ability will be shamed for showing 'weakness'. The children learn that they must abandon what they really think and feel to play these roles.

Lack of trust

At a fundamental level, children in both roles know they cannot trust their parent. Instead they have to remain vigilant of the parent. They cannot trust their parent to have their back if they turn their attention elsewhere. The narcissistic parent demands their constant attention in this respect. A child cannot trust an adult they have to keep watch over lest that adult hurt them.

Lack of attention

Children in both roles are deprived of the attention to their authentic selves they need. Instead, they are forced to attend to the narcissistic parent's inflated self. That self is supposed to be most important and entitled to others' attention and support at all times. Children in both roles can come away believing that others' needs are more important than their own.

> As Marcia grew, it was clear that Sharon expected her to be available at all times. Marcia knew not to make good friends or have sources of happiness unrelated to her mother.
>
> Marcia had to cut off her own desires from her awareness. She could not let herself know how much she wanted to prioritize friends as she entered adolescence. She saw how much her brother angered her mother by wanting to see his friends and she did not want that same fate.
>
> Marcia devised a system to manage her mother's emotional demands. She saw keeping her mother happy as a game. She just had to do and say the right things, and she could win this game. For Marcia, this meant figuring out what would make her mother happy and doing it ahead of time. She would clean the house and do the dishes without being asked. She silently vowed never to complain to her mother.
>
> She felt lonely but did not know why. She had no one to tell how she was honestly feeling. She had a nagging sense that no one really knew her. If they did, she was certain they would be disappointed.
>
> As Matt grew he learned to expect opposition from his mother at every turn. If he wanted see his friends his

mother would come up with a list of chores he had not yet done. He could only go see them after the chores but it would be too late by then. Over time, he grew weary of trying to fight her for his freedoms. He stopped asking her if he could go to parties in eighth grade because he knew she would say 'No'.

He also knew never to ask his mother for anything. She already called him 'selfish' regularly. Asking her for help with anything in his life would only evoke more of this reaction. He learned to ignore his own needs because expressing them only led to humiliation.

Matt, too, felt lonely. He could not tell his father about his mother's hostility. He would only blame Matt for angering his mother. Matt was confused about who he really was. His friends seemed to like him but he was always 'doing something wrong' to make his mother angry at him. He assumed his mother must know him best and that his friends only liked him because they did not know him like she did.

How the scapegoat and golden child roles are pitted against each other

It is in the narcissistic parent's interest for the scapegoat child and golden child to not get along. The parent insists on a reality where the scapegoat child deserves the parent's wrath. Similarly, the parent has to seem deserving of the golden child's admiration and affiliation.

The golden child who witnesses the narcissistic parent devaluing the scapegoat child must make sense of this. And they must do so in a way that leads them to conclude their parent is correct in their actions. They have to perceive the scapegoat child as 'bad'. If the parent is always right then the scapegoat child is bad for angering them. This can lead to the golden child seeing and treating the scapegoat child the same way as the parent.

The scapegoat child can experience the golden child to be yet another adversary in the family. They seem to be doing everything perfect and getting praised by the person who persecutes the scapegoat child. This can build resentment. The golden child may echo the parent's accusations and derision. These efforts may be intended to get the scapegoat child to do what the parent asks so they will not get attacked. Nonetheless, the scapegoat child may see this as just another attack by a family member.

> *Marcia and Matt grew apart during adolescence. Marcia could not figure out why he would not just 'play the game' so their mother would not attack him. Matt wished that Marcia could see there was no way to win this game. It was rigged against him. Matt thought Marcia loved being her mother's favorite. It made him angry that she would be so allied with someone who treated him so poorly. Marcia wished Matt knew how coerced she felt to be her mother's ally. She had no other choice.*

Their brick porch told the whole story. During the summer, whenever Matt wanted to go meet his friends, his mother would often tell him that he had to scrape the moss off of this brick porch first. This was painstaking work. He had to take a paint scraper, get on his hands and knees and scrape the moss from the grout between the bricks. It required a good three hours to do the whole porch. He would complain that it was not fair to have to do this but his mother was unmoved. Matt knew he hated doing this chore but his mother was forcing him to.

Marcia saw scraping the brick porch differently. She knew that this was something her mother wanted. All she had to do was complete this chore, and she would advance to another stage in the 'game' that her life had to be about. She felt compelled to wake up one morning and get to scraping the brick porch herself. It took her the full three hours. Her hands and knees were aching afterward. When her mother returned home from shopping that day, she saw the porch and showered Marcia with praise.

Neither Matt nor Marcia got to choose what they wanted in their lives. Matt could not choose to see his friends because his mother would actively prevent him. Marcia could not choose anything that might displease her mother. She had to convince herself that she wanted whatever it was that made her mother happy. This included "deciding" to scrape the brick porch.

Possibilities for reconciliation

After surviving a childhood as the scapegoat, one may want to connect with their sibling over what they went through. The scapegoat survivor may find it relatively easier to see their parent as troubled. They were free to know their complaints about this parent growing up. The survivor may yearn to ally with their sibling to validate each other's experience of their abusive parent.

The scapegoat survivor's yearning may run into the golden survivor's forced loyalty to the parent. In contrast to the scapegoat child, the golden child faced more pressure to approve of all the parent did. This had to be the child's identity in the eyes of the parent. To challenge the parent in the way the scapegoat survivor wants may threaten the golden child survivor's sense of their own identity. As a result the golden child survivor may rebuff the scapegoat survivor's efforts to come together and heal from the abuse.

The laissez-faire principle

If a scapegoat survivor runs into this type of reception from their golden child survivor sibling there is little to be done. The scapegoat survivor seems faced with the choice of trying to convince their sibling that their childhood was not what it should have been or surrender this hope and work with what is within their control. This may mean creating psychological distance with this sibling so that the wish for their validation is more easily surrendered.

Laissez-faire is a policy or attitude of letting things take their own course without interfering. This approach can be helpfully applied to navigating the sibling relationship after childhood. The scapegoat survivor can resolve not to try to change the perspective of the golden child sibling. Similarly, the golden child survivor can resolve not to insist that the scapegoat survivor change their perspective. At the same time, the scapegoat survivor would do whatever they need to do to continue healing from this abuse. This would include putting the three pillars of recovery into action.

As time passes, the golden child survivor may - or may not - come to their own conclusion that something was amiss in their childhood home. If that day comes, then the scapegoat survivor and golden child survivor may be able to witness for each other what they endured. If that day does not come then neither party will be trying to force something to happen that is out of their control.

> *When Matt was 55 years old he got an email out of the blue from Marcia. They had agreed not to talk about their upbringing and kept interactions to be infrequent and on the surface. On this day, however, he read that Marcia could see what he had been saying about their mother. She explained that she had started her own course of therapy. In it she realized how she was weaponized against Matt. She sincerely apologized for*

persisting their mother's attitude towards him in adulthood.

Matt was blown away by this email. He was so grateful to finally have his sister on his side. They started to talk on the phone, and he readily accepted her apology. They got to rebuild their relationships based on the truth of what they survived.

Matt learned more about what it was really like for Marcia. He was taken with compassion to know that Marcia had to voluntarily scrape the back porch.

He said to her, "You know, I was treated like a second-class citizen for all to see in the family. But in that, at least I could complain - even to myself - and know that I did not like being treated that way. It's different - but no less insidious - for you. Almost like getting hooked on heroin from an early age. Our mother shot you up with praise from the start. You had no choice but to grow addicted to it at the expense of your own free will. To have to supposedly choose to scrape that back porch shows this. I wish you did not have to go through that."

Marcia had not thought about the costs to her of 'playing the game' that Matt was pointing out. It felt right to her, though.

I want to emphasize that reconciliation may not be in the cards like this for many siblings. That can be something to be accepted in the course of your recovery. There is still a lot of life to live if this does not happen.

8

Three Ways the Narcissistic Parent Blocks the Scapegoat Child's Growth

> *As a child, did you feel...*
> *...like everything you did was wrong?*
> *...like there was an aching hole inside that never seemed to fill up?*
> *...like you were not allowed to have good relationships outside of your family?*

Scapegoat children to narcissistic parents are familiar with such experiences. They are used to being known as someone defective and undeserving. The scapegoat child gets devalued, deprived, and controlled by the narcissistic parent. The net impact is to prevent the child from growing and developing.

Narcissistic parents exploit their children

In a family headed by a narcissistic parent, the children get exploited. Some, like the golden child, are used to promote that parent's inflated self-worth. The parent's logic goes, "I am superior because my child reflects who I am." Others, like the scapegoat child are used to suffer that parent's self-hatred. The parent's logic goes, "I am superior because my child does not reflect who I am."

The narcissistic parent pressures the scapegoat child and the golden child to agree with the treatment they receive. A golden child must participate in a mutual admiration society with the parent - or else.

> *Marcia always thought she was the apple of her mother's eye. Her mother would take her shopping every weekend. They would try on clothes together and get ice cream. Upon arriving home, her mother would invariably find a reason to yell at her older brother Matt. For instance, she might claim that he had left something out in the kitchen and this meant he did not respect her. She would say that he was irresponsible and selfish and send him to his room as punishment. Marcia would 'check out' in such moments. She did not like seeing her brother treated this way. He seemed to be a good person. She felt something very strong pulling her to agree with her mother. She knew something would tear the fabric of the family apart if she did not go along with her mother.*

Marcia felt extreme - yet subtle - pressure to agree with her mother's perspective. In retrospect it was the only reality her mother offered her. Marcia and her mother were the special people and Matt was the lowly 'bad' child. To question this arrangement would be to occupy a different reality than her mother. That would have been too psychologically dangerous for any child to do.

The scapegoat child also has to conform to the narcissistic parent's reality. This child embodies the narcissistic parent's intolerable feelings of inadequacy. They project these feelings onto the scapegoat child. The parent then influences that child to experience these feelings as their own. The child feels like the worthless one because there is no other way to be in the parent's reality.

The consequences for the scapegoat child's development can be severe.

Three ways the narcissistic parent interrupts the scapegoat child's growth

The scapegoat child is deprived, devalued and controlled by the narcissistic parent.

1) Deprivation of emotional nourishment

To grow, all children need to feel encouraged and attended to by their parent. This lets the child know they continue to exist when they show their increasing capabilities. Children with 'good-enough' parents feel a sense of continuity with themselves as they grow. They get to enjoy the feelings of power that come along with growth without sacrificing connection to important others.

The scapegoat child finds nobody around when they seek recognition and affirmation for their growth. Without these responses they do not have the necessary support needed to grow. Instead of getting to enjoy their development, the scapegoat child feel more lonely and unloved.

A prominent psychoanalyst named James Masterson calls this the 'abandonment depression' (1975). He describes how children of narcissistic parents can feel worse when they demonstrate their capabilities. They were painfully deprived of the parental responsiveness needed to support their growth. As a result, expressions of competence by a scapegoat survivor as an adult can feel similarly painful.

> *Donald was born to a narcissistic mother and a passive father. He came to therapy in his mid-20's to address anxiety and feelings of emptiness. Donald presented as an athletic, well-kempt, intelligent, articulate and professionally successful young man. As therapy proceeded Donald confessed that he did not feel like he owned any of these personal qualities.*
>
> *As a a child, Donald had to orbit his mother who was prone to violent rages if she did not feel obeyed and admired at all times. He had no recollection of getting to occupy the center of the family's attention in his childhood. At least not in a positive way. As a result he kept his growth as a person a secret to himself and to his family. For example, neither parent asked him about romantic partners or acknowledged that as a teenager*

he would be appropriately looking to date. Without anyone noticing and encouraging Donald's development he did not have a way to identify with himself. Instead he had to identify with his mother's imposed upon identity as the defective and undeserving family scapegoat. All of this led to him being struck by feelings of panic when a woman showed interest in him. Although he knew he wanted this attention in theory, in practice it made him feel endangered and he did not know why.

Donald's case demonstrates the abandonment depression he would experience when he tried to take ownership of qualities as a person. He coped by feeling dissociated from himself and seeing his abilities as fraudulent. This can be a consequence of the emotional deprivation faced by the scapegoat child.

2) Devaluation of the scapegoat child

The narcissistic parent perceives and treats the scapegoat child to be worth less than everyone else in the family. This child has to believe in their devalued status to share a reality with the family. The arrangement lets the parent feel better than the child by comparison.

The child may cope with the parent's devaluation by adopting the unconscious belief that they are defective. If the scapegoat child is defective then what is the point to growing? Becoming an even bigger defect? This is one of the tragic consequences for the scapegoat child.

Steve was the scapegoat to his narcissistic father. At home he could never do anything right according to his father. If Steve folded his clothes and put them in his dresser his father would storm into his room, accuse him of shoddy work and dump the clothes on the floor for him to re-fold. Such occurrences were common and led Steve to conclude that he was defective. As he grew up he found other ways to convince himself of his defectiveness. He believed himself to be unathletic despite playing several sports. He thought that he was going to fail the next assignment in his advanced classes despite having good grades. He could not think of himself without simultaneously thinking of something that was - supposedly - wrong with him.

Steve could not know himself in any way that was positive. To do so would have been to defy his father's narrative of him. As poorly as his father would treat him, Steve felt something much worse would be in store if he saw himself as having worth. Doing so would have prevented his father from using him to embody his own worthlessness. He knew deep down that his father would never stand for that and would likely attack Steve even more. That was the 'something worse' he feared.

3) Controlling the scapegoat child

The scapegoat child's valued relationships threaten the narcissistic parent. If the scapegoat child finds friendships and relationships that they value and with whom they feel valued then they may question the narcissistic parent's devaluation. The child can absorb the parent's cast off feelings of inadequacy to the extent they feel deserving of them. Thus, a child's good relationships are often a threat to the narcissistic parent.

Such parents will seek and try to destroy the scapegoat child's valued relationships. The parent may use punishments to prevent the scapegoat child from participating in friendships. Similarly, romantic relationships may be undermined by the narcissistic parent.

To cope, the scapegoat child may have to sever connections to people they care about. This strategy spares the child the pain of having the narcissistic parent take these relationships away. However it costs the child the kinds of relationships needed to counter the narcissistic parent's devaluation. That is exactly why the narcissistic parent seeks to take them away.

Matt recalled a moment he lost a potential friendship because of his mother. As a sophomore in high school he worked at a car wash with a friend named Rick who was a senior. One day after their shift, Rick asked Matt if he wanted to come watch the Detroit Lions game at his house on Sunday? Matt felt a surge of good feeling. Rick had never asked him to hang out socially. He was an older kid too. This must mean he thinks I'm cool. Matt said he would be there.

As Matt pedaled his bike home he grew extremely nervous about telling his mother his plans. He feared she would not let him go. Tragically he was right. He told her about Rick's invitation and she said, "Oh, you're not going! They're going to be drinking beer there. It's no place for a 10th grader." Matt was not sure where she drew her conclusions but there was no speaking back to her.

Matt had to make up an excuse to Rick the next day for why he could not go. He was too embarrassed to say his mother would not let him. Rick said, "ah, next time." Matt found himself hoping he would not ask again so Matt would not have to make up another excuse. He knew his mother would never let him go. Matt began subtly distancing himself from Rick at their job. Over time they drifted apart.

Matt's narcissistic mother thwarted his attempts to find sources of happiness outside the family. This left Matt feeling trapped. Psychologically speaking he was chained to his family's home.

How to resume growth

The three pillars of recovery all point to this question. By making sense of what happened so you know it was not your fault you can realize how the past 'facts' were false. You did not deserve to be devalued, deprived nor controlled by your narcissistic parent.

By gaining distance from your narcissistic abuser your system gets more and more information that you are now safe. That safety can make it easier to get closer to people who are safe. Closer connections to people who are safe will allow you to know that your own growth will not compromise these relationships.

By living in defiance of the narcissist's rules for living you are engaging in bold acts of growth. Maybe you take up a sport that you gave up in adolescence and take note of your abilities in it. Perhaps you join a choir to resume the singing talent you had to hide from your narcissistic parent. Maybe you invite your friends and partners to your performance. They get to cheer you on as you display your true developed self. All of this is in defiance of the narcissist's rules and promotes your conclusion that you will not be deprived, devalued nor controlled when you move forward in your life.

9

Invisible to a Narcissistic Parent

> *Have you ever felt overlooked and unseen by a narcissistic parent?*
> *Has it seemed like your narcissistic parent already knew everything there was to know about you?*
> *Despite feeling invisible to this parent, have you felt guilty if you don't tend to their needs?*

Children of a narcissistic parent are often deprived of feeling visible. A narcissistic parent is not curious about the child's inner world. They are too busy propping up their own and using others to aid this purpose. The child ends up feeling invisible to the parent.

Despite this invisibility, the child has to forge some way of relating to this parent. In other words, the child has to find a way to be somebody to this parent even though they feel like nobody to them. This involves suppressing the pain of feeling invisible and forcing themselves to fit into the parent's world. The narcissistic parent will use the child to boost their inflated yet fragile self-esteem. This can mean serving as a caricatured ally or enemy to the parent. Either role yields no genuine feeling of visibility to this parent.

3 ways children feel invisible to the narcissistic parent

A narcissistic parent believes children exist to serve their needs. The parent is justified because they see their own needs as most important. The child is left feeling invisible to this parent. It is as if the children are put on a shelf in the narcissistic parent's mind, only to be taken down when it suits the parent. Otherwise, the child is expected to remain silent.

Here are three ways a narcissistic parent might make a child feel invisible:

#1: Getting ignored

The narcissistic parent may regard their ambitions as supremely important. Whatever or whoever serves to facilitate these ambitions is worth the parent's time. Conditions or people who do not further the parent's ambitions are worthless to them. Children often fall into the latter category. They can feel like they do not matter unless they fit into the parent's sphere of self-interest.

> *Sandya's father was absorbed in his work. He prioritized whatever he thought would help him get ahead and saw fatherhood as a distant second. He would arrive home just before dinnertime then retire to his office immediately afterwards to keep working. He did not involve himself in his wife or children's lives.*

Sandya knew from a young age not to approach her father with any emotional need. If she felt scared and cried out for him he would act like he did not hear her. If she was joyous and wanted to share this with him he would seem preoccupied with something else.

As Sandya grew older she realized that if she asked her father about his work then he would pay some attention to her. She google'd the name of her father's company and read up on it. She made a list of questions in her mind to ask him when he got home that night. To her surprise he seemed happy that she was interested in his work. For the first time in her life he did not seem impatient in his dealings with her. He spoke to her for a full 30 minutes as she made sure to show enthusiasm and interest in what he was telling her.

In this example, Sandya was inconsequential to her father until she reflected what was most important to him. She felt invisible unless she was applauding him.

#2: Shining a favorable light

The narcissistic parent may anoint a child as the supposed best. This serves the parent's needs by affording them more admiration. The child's excellence in the parent's eyes reflects more on the parent than the child. Treating a child in this way reinforces the parent's fragile claim on their own superiority.

This can be very confusing for the child. Nothing they can do is seemingly wrong in the parent's eyes. Yet the parent may find everything wrong with other people in their orbit. The child knows that they are not perfect and wonders what the parent would do if they knew this. The child may feel celebrated but invisible to the narcissistic parent.

> *Marcia was always her mother's favorite. She would accompany her on shopping trips where her mother would try on different clothes and ask for Marcia's opinion. Her mother would turn to Marcia for validation after yelling at her scapegoat brother. Marcia felt very special to her mother. As she grew older, however, Marcia began to feel like she led a double life. Her friends at school started cursing and being interested in boys. She feared that her mother would disown her if she knew about this side of her. All that seemed visible to her mother was Marcia's supposed perfection. Her fallibility went invisible and so did Marcia's sense of being a real person to her mother.*

#3: Throwing you under the bus

A narcissistic parent may also only see negative qualities in a child. This serves the parent's needs by getting to feel superior by virtue of being unlike this child. The parent relocates their own sense of worthlessness into this child and then gets the child to identify with it. In order for this to work the parent and child have to believe that there is nothing good about the child.

This, of course, feels terrible for the child put into this role of scapegoat. They also feel invisible because it is an artificiality. The parts of them that are good - which may be substantial - cannot exist to the parent. The scapegoat child is left confused how nothing about them seems to please their parent. They are left feeling like only their badness is visible to the parent. Their goodness feels invisible to both of them.

> Matt was Marcia's older brother. He got the opposite treatment from their narcissistic mother. She was always harping on Matt about something. He hadn't cleaned his room like she asked. He was slouching. He was chewing too loudly. He was mumbling. At every turn she found fault in how he conducted himself. Seeing her treat his sister so well told Matt that his mother had the capacity to be kind but she did not see him as worthy.
>
> At school Matt was well-liked by his peers, a good athlete in sports and got good grades. These facts about him seemed meaningless to his mother. It was as if his good qualities were invisible to her. This made him question the value of these qualities. If his own mother did not think they mattered then why should he? He grew to see himself as worthless in the way she was influencing him to.

How children survive by living narrowly

Children are highly motivated to avoid the experience of being invisible. The cost of going unseen by their parent can feel like being nobody to no one. This is an agonizing experience that we must avoid at all costs. If it cannot be avoided then the effects must be numbed.

Having to be who you are not

One way the child of a narcissistic parent may avoid or manage feeling invisible is to constrict themselves to be who the parent sees.

> *Marcia grew to see herself as perfect - or having to be perfect - in the same way her mother saw her. As a result, her human fallibility felt like an unpardonable sin. If she got anything but an A on a school assignment she would feel a torrent of self-loathing and want to inflict pain on herself. She never shared these feelings with anyone. She was too ashamed to admit how she did not fit into her mother's view of her.*

> *Matt had a different problem. He could not see anything good about being who he was. He was only visible to his mother when he was messing up, in need of correction, or a source of irritation. His victories, attributes and decency had no place in how she knew him. He found himself always finding a problem with everything he did. A good grade was a fluke. Friendly receptions were*

evidence the person did not really know him. He gravitated towards friends and partners who saw him the way he was seen at home.

Marcia and Matt had to constrict themselves in similar ways and with grave costs. Living this way still spared them the far worse experience of feeling unknown to their parent.

Having to be a ghost

The child who goes ignored may constrict their awareness of themselves entirely. To be aware of themselves is to know and feel a tormenting problem with no solution - that they are not somebody to their parent. So, they figure out how to be a ghost to themselves.

The child can feel invisible even when in the presence of the parent. They may not be spoken to or acknowledged in any way. If the child takes offense to how little they seem to matter to this parent, they will only suffer more. The narcissistic parent may humiliate the child for not being self-sufficient or lash out at them for not reflecting back their perfect parenting.

Under such conditions the only way to survive is to constrict their awareness. The child may go off in their mind to be occupied with anything but the painful reality in front of them. They may push themselves out of their minds and seek to be the ghost they are treated as.

Sandya conditioned herself to make do with her father's inability to care about her existence. She did not make demands on him. She did whatever she could to avoid irritating him. This meant being very careful to clean up after herself even as a young child. Otherwise her father's ignorance of her would be interrupted by his gruff angry scolding for being so messy. It was one of the few times he reacted directly to her and it hurt. Over time, she found that living hurt a lot less when she focused on anyone and anything other than herself.

Relationships where you are visible

To heal from being invisible to a narcissistic parent, survivors need to find and participate in relationships where they are readily visible. This is not always easy.

If you survived a childhood of feeling invisible you may not know anything different. Worse, you may be conditioned to avoid visibility to others given how bad it has felt in the past. That is why the process of healing is a long one.

The survivor is working to recover a loving and respectful relationship with all of themselves. To do this, they must stay in connection with the parts of themselves that were invisible to their parent. This means incrementally tolerating the shame, self-loathing, and despair that used to go with visibility. In order for this exercise to be productive the survivor has to do it in the context of a new safe relationship. Reinforcement from another person is needed for the survivor's attempts to be visible.

It can be hard to find such safe relationships initially. As I described earlier, the expectation for invisibility can lead one to find relationships that comply. If you are wary of your current ability to find safe relationships then psychotherapy is a good option.

Therapy is one place where you have very high odds of finding a safe relationship. This lets the survivor control for the variable of whether the other person is safe. Now if the survivor of invisibility does not feel safe or visible there is a chance to explore what is happening. Of course, the therapist may have actually done, said, or not done something that led to this. Most therapists can earnestly and non-defensively explore this possibility. Alternatively, the survivor's feelings of danger may be holdovers from what being visible used to mean. In these cases the survivor gets to feel understood by someone else for what they used to have to endure privately. They can talk about how and what is making them feel endangered in that moment. As they are met with implicit compassion and validation, the danger lessens.

Over time - sometimes significant amounts of time - the survivor may find it appealing to be visible. The post-traumatic consequences of being invisible to their narcissistic parent may have subsided. Now, they welcome the opportunity to see themselves fully and be seen by certain others.

Sandya came to therapy in her mid-twenties because she felt like she was just going through the motions in her life. She fell into states of depression on the weekends when she was not working. She described feeling like a stranger to herself and unable to find meaning on her own.

She and I would work together for several years. During this time, I understood how inconsequential she felt to her father. I would highlight to her how she operated from this assumption currently. I would also show her whenever possible that she mattered to me as a client. So, Sandya found insight into the way her father's self-absorption impacted her. She also received current information in the therapeutic relationship that contradicted her conclusion that she did not matter to others. These two factors worked in tandem over the years to restore her sense of her own visibility to others and herself.

10

When the Scapegoat Has to Deny Their Own Gifts

> *Is it much easier to celebrate others' accomplishments than your own?*
> *Do you feel most uncomfortable when receiving praise?*
> *Do you presume that you do not deserve anyone's praise?*

Being the scapegoat child to a narcissistic parent means feeling very unimportant. You may have even felt like you did not exist to this parent. Psychologically speaking you would not be wrong.

It is very painful for a child to attach to a parent who does not see nor care about the child's existence. The rule is that the parent is more important than the child. Therefore the child's resulting anguish at feeling devalued and deprived is inconsequential.

In this arrangement, the child avoids experiences that reflect their importance. Such experience contradicts the narcissistic parent's rule that they are unimportant. The child can feel worse in such moments. They have to painfully know what they are missing out on. The injustice of their arrangement and its permanence can agonize them.

One of the ways a scapegoat child risks feeling important is in their gifts. We all have gifts. Whether it is singing, writing, athletics, connecting to others, etc. When someone outside the family sees and celebrates the scapegoat child's gifts, the child is in a difficult position. They need to protect themselves from the pain of knowing what they are missing. And the child risks the narcissistic parent's vindictive attack if their gifts evoke that parent's envy.

In this case, the child has to deny their own gifts and learn to celebrate others' gifts instead of their own. Both strategies protect the child. The scapegoat survivor may unconsciously continue to deny their gifts by finding relationships with other narcissists. Later, survivors can find it safe to recover their gifts in new relationships.

The dangers of the scapegoat child owning their gifts

#1: Being important when you're not supposed to be

The scapegoat child's gifts threaten the required arrangement with the narcissistic parent. The child is assumed to be - and treated as - less important than the narcissistic parent. The child getting recognized as special or gifted is not part of this equation.

There are two ways the narcissistic parent enforces this disparity. The parent's self-absorption denies the child of the recognition that they matter. By extension, their gifts cannot matter. This context makes the child's recognition of their gifts feel all the more painful.

Alyssa was eight years old and trying out for her softball little league team. She remembered coming to the plate where a coach was pitching to the players. The goal was to see how well the players hit to see who would go to which team. Alyssa had only played tee-ball before this and was a decent but not great hitter then.

She got to the plate and the first pitch she saw she crushed into the opposite outfield. "What just happened?" she excitedly asked herself. The coach said, "Wow!" and said he was going to throw another one. <<Pop!>> the ball rocketed off her bat into centerfield and over the outfielder's head. And so it went. She had no idea this was in her.

As the tryout practice was wrapping up, her coach said, "Well I guess we know who's going to be the #1 pick in this year's softball league draft," as he nodded to Alyssa. Alyssa was over the moon yet felt a tinge of worry. These were unfamiliar feelings. She was not used to being singled out for good reasons. She was the scapegoat child in her family. Her father was wholly disinterested in her except when he criticized her about something. Her mother was volatile and prone to yell at Alyssa at the drop of a hat.

Alyssa looked towards the dugout and saw her father there to pick her up. The coach came over to him and said, "Your daughter is something else! She hit the ball out of the park all practice." He looked at Alyssa and she felt intensely uncomfortable. Something was wrong.

As they walked to his car, Alyssa found herself offering herself up for his critique. "Dad, what did you think of my form when I was hitting the ball? Was it OK?". This gave her father something she unconsciously knew he required. "Well, your elbow kept sagging down. You need to make sure to keep it up." Alyssa stopped and tried to mimic the form he described and said, "You mean, like this?". "Yes, exactly," she said.

From that moment on, Alyssa found herself obsessing over whether she had the right batting stance or not. So much so, that she was too preoccupied to hit the ball like she did during tryouts. To stay less important than her narcissistic father she had to present herself as faulty to him. This let him feel superior as the one who could tell her how to fix herself.

Alyssa felt tension at being recognized for being able to hit in front of a parent who denied her importance. The gulf of how her coach responded to her versus her father's typical indifference towards her was distressing. She coped by sacrificing her gift into something that needed correction by her 'all-knowing' father. She lost her right to enjoy this gift but restored the order required in her family.

One of the ways a scapegoat child can keep their morale up in such a dreadful situation is to tell themselves that the parent will eventually recognize their importance if they follow this rule. Alyssa did this by assuming she would hit even better if she mastered her father's recommendation.

#2: Evoking the narcissistic parent's envy

The second danger of the scapegoat child owning their gifts is making the narcissistic parent envious. Envy is a feeling of inadequacy due to seeing someone possess something you do not. Next, is the desire to destroy that person's possession so you feel more adequate. This is a frequent experience for narcissistic people.

Scapegoat survivors of narcissistic parents recall being punished suspiciously soon after a success. Kids who were popular at school and invited to sleep over at friends' homes would often return the next morning to a parent irate at them. The reasons could vary but the sequence was the same. A child who announces they won a spelling contest in school at the dinner table might get criticized for their table manners a few moments later.

The scapegoat child learns to associate the parent's vindictive attack with their successes. As a matter of protection, the child must deny their gifts. Sure, it is painful but it beats being attacked all the time.

How the scapegoat child copes

Although it is too dangerous to own their gifts, the scapegoat child can celebrate others' gifts. There are several benefits to this coping strategy. It often comes naturally for such children to empathize with and promote others' gifts. When directed towards the narcissistic parent the child can buy themselves some protection. By celebrating the parent's gifts, the child is seeing the parent as more important. This prevents the parent from feeling envious and attacking the child.

Celebrating others' gifts instead of one's own is often welcome by others. It is generally a good quality to appreciate others' gifts. A scapegoat child may have a generosity of spirit in this regard.

The challenge is the rule that the child not accept the same appreciation in return. The scapegoat child is left feeling appreciated for celebrating others' gifts while being forbidden from being celebrated. This can leave the child feeling privately exploited and empty. They feel appreciated for what they give but not for who they are. Their only reliable sense of worth can be making others' feel good about their gifts.

How scapegoat survivors continue denying their gifts

The child can become occupied with the fantasy of the parent's eventual change of heart. This makes the narcissistic parent's actual punishments of the child for expressing their gifts to be something that has to be endured before the bliss of being loved. In fact, this sort of mistreatment can get associated with the supposed promise of love to follow.

In this way the scapegoat child believes that things are not what they seem. The narcissistic parent's envy, withholding, and vindictiveness is a pit stop on the way to something much better. This is necessary for the child to believe while dependent on the narcissistic parent. It would be disastrous to know that what they see is what they get from the narcissistic parent. The parent does not have a chamber inside them full of love that the child can unlock. If they did, the child would have already received it. This can only be understood and known with enough distance from the parent.

The scapegoat survivor can later feel strongly attracted to similar narcissistic people. When they find someone who is threatened by their gifts the survivor can associate this with the promise of love. A partner who denies their gifts is offering helpful correction. With enough self-modification, the partner may give them the acceptance they seek. Things are not what they seem in such relationships. The fantasy that helped the survivor survive their narcissistic parent leads them toward similar predicaments.

The path to recovering your gifts

A scapegoat survivor needs to experience firsthand an ongoing relationship where their gifts do not threaten it. In a relationship with someone who is safe, the danger of them turning away or against you is not present. Expression of your gifts does not evoke withdrawal or hostility from the other. With repetition the association between being gifted and being endangered diminishes.

It is not the experience of using one's gifts that is the problem. Rather it is the traumatic association of these gifts with the narcissistic parent's retaliation that is the problem. In new relationships, the survivor experiences an entirely different calculus. They receive care and attention for being who they are, not for how they meet the other's needs.

The scapegoat survivor has to shift from valuing the promise of love to whether it is present. Instead of seeing love and acceptance as something that comes after feeling undeserving, the survivor gets to expect it now. If the survivor is not given the acceptance they seek then this is a signal to look elsewhere. This means taking the other person's treatment of you at face value. You get to prize the actual presence of being treated well rather than its promise.

A common challenge in this process is feeling guilty for moving away from people who do not treat you well. This may seem hard to understand at face value. If you were the scapegoat child then you had to take responsibility for the narcissistic parent's emotional well-being. That was the parent's entitled expectation of you. Failure to do so would result in further suffering for the child. As a result, the survivor's decision to move away from people who mistreat them can feel like shirking their responsibility. Guilt is soon to follow.

A way to challenge and move past such guilt is to remind yourself that you are only responsible for your emotional well-being. This is easier said than experienced. It is important to gain new experience in relationships that endorse this point. Spend time with people who prioritize their own needs so that others are not expected to. This arrangement means that neither party has to abandon themselves to take care of the other person. Part of caring for your own emotional well-being can include expressing your gifts.

11

Fear of Growing Up for Scapegoat Survivors of Narcissistic Parents

> *As an adult in chronological age do you still feel much younger?*
> *Do you defer to authorities even in matters where you have expertise?*
> *Do you feel undeserving of others' respect and admiration?*

Scapegoat survivors of narcissistic parents often feel different than their peers. They experience themselves to have less authority than other adults. They may feel much younger than their chronological age. They may feel less knowledgeable, less powerful, and less worthy of admiration.

It can be tempting to label this experience as 'low self-esteem' and keep moving. I think there is something much different happening. The scapegoat child learns that their existence depends on being less powerful than their narcissistic parent. So they must actively thwart, deny and avoid their own power. Growing up inherently means becoming more powerful. To protect themselves the child may develop a distrust, fear and suspiciousness of their own power. Doing so keeps them in relationship to the narcissistic parent in the only way that parent allows.

The narcissistic parent's need to domineer their child

A narcissistic parent often domineers the people they have the most authority over. Children become frequent victims. To domineer is to 'assert one's will over another in an arrogant way'.

The narcissistic parent benefits from domineering by feeling powerful. It is an artificial and unearned sense of power but that is of little consequence. Their need to always 'be on top' may reflect their own core sense of powerlessness. Instead of acknowledging these feelings they unconsciously deny them. Next, the narcissistic parent psychologically relocates these feelings into someone else. It is not enough to just see someone else as powerless - they must influence that person to adopt these powerless feelings as their own.

A narcissistic parent easily gets their scapegoat child to identify as the powerless one. Limiting the child's freedoms in a 'because I said so' kind of way leaves the child in an amoral and powerless world. The child learns that their wishes have no standing with their parent. The child's ability to do what they want to do rests on the whim of their parent. And the parent's whims are always at odds with the child's desire to feel in charge of themselves. In this way the child lives in a dictatorship as a forced subject.

Ira's father treated him like he was a servant from an early age. He never asked Ira to do a task. He issued commands. "Take these trays to the trash can," he would order Ira as they finished up their lunch at Burger King. "Set the table for dinner." "Get my shoes."

Ira recalled balking a few times when his father did this. He felt bossed around and it was infuriating. He also knew he had to be careful of his father's temper. It was not OK to say 'No' to this man. Ira knew he could face a wrath that he was not prepared for. Instead Ira would try to eke out some say in the matter by trying to do things on his timeline. He tried, "OK, give me five minutes." This was not enough submission for his domineering father. He barked, "What did you say? You're going to do something when I tell you to do it. Not later. NOW!" Ira recalled how it was one thing to be told this and another to see the heartless contempt in his father's eyes towards him. Ira felt an intolerable mix of rage at this injustice and shame at being so emotionally estranged from his parent. No child could navigate such feelings on their own so he would do what was necessary to make them go away. He would do what his father ordered.

Why submission is the only option for the scapegoat child

The scapegoat child's ability to tolerate seeming powerless helps them survive. The narcissistic parent threatens the child in three ways. First, they dictate the terms under which they will recognize the child as being their child. If the child determines they only get to be their narcissistic parent's child by being powerless then so be it. It is far better than going unrecognized by their parent. Second, the child's expressions of power can draw even more abuse from the parent. Third, the child's pain of being emotionally abandoned gets temporarily relieved by living as their parent needs them to.

The narcissistic parent only recognizes the scapegoat child as someone at their mercy. For the child, getting recognized by their parent is mandatory. If the child were to insist on their freedoms they would risk being someone the parent cannot tolerate to be close to. This can result in the unsurvivable state of being nobody to no one for the child.

A narcissistic parent will enforce the scapegoat child's powerlessness via threat and coercion. The narcissistic parent can only feel powerful when the scapegoat child seems powerless. If the child does not go along with this then the parent is at risk of feeling their own feelings of powerlessness. That is unacceptable to a narcissistic parent. If or when the child attempts to recover their own sense of power the parent will undermine the child all the more. Many scapegoat survivors recall the worst emotional and physical attacks happened when they questioned their parent's authority.

In the midst of all of this psychological manipulation and exploitation, the child's actual self is abandoned. This is unrelentingly painful. The child learns that complying with their parent's insistence on being all-powerful yields some relief from this pain. If or when the child loses hope of their parent ever granting them a measure of respect they can cope by living as though the parent's needs are the child's. Now if the parent seems content then the child can too. This strategy requires the child to dissociate from their own experience.

> *Ira recalled feeling different from his friends from an early age. He felt like he was headed towards somewhere dark in his future. Other boys his age seemed to revel in their newfound strengths or abilities. Ira could sit back and support those friends but could not feel this way about himself.*
>
> *In the seventh grade, he was deathly afraid of his father finding out that he was becoming interested in girls. This felt like an embarrassing secret he had to keep. He also had to make sure his father did not know too much about certain friends. The ones that acted with freedom and liked to get into mischief appealed to Ira. But if his father knew that he was keeping company with such free spirits then he would make up a reason for why Ira was not allowed to see them.*

Ira's attempts to live as an adolescent were rebuked by his father. Ira knew that he faced something terrible within if he grew up. That 'something terrible' was becoming someone that his father would not and could not recognize.

The threat of the child's growth to the narcissistic parent

The narcissistic parent's supposed right to domineer the scapegoat child is built on flimsy evidence. Usually, it is something like "I'm the parent." Since the parent is older and grown up they have a right to control the younger and less developed child.

This weak foundation of dominance is severely threatened by the child's increasing age and maturity. Now both parties are at risk of not recognizing each other. The child had to get used to being domineered to feel like they were somebody to someone. The parent has staved off their own powerlessness for so long in this arrangement that they can feel terrified at not being able to stow this feeling in their child. In order to keep being someone to the parent and to protect that parent from feeling their own powerlessness the child can develop unconscious beliefs that find fault with how they are growing up.

The scapegoat child's beliefs that interfere with growing up

The scapegoat child of a domineering narcissistic parent may have to deny their entrance into the adult world. The threats of being nobody to no one, attack from the narcissistic parent and/or the pain of emotional abandonment demand this. Here are two beliefs that serve to cripple the scapegoat survivor's sense of being a full-fledged adult.

"I don't deserve to be loved when I leave childhood"

A domineering narcissistic parent may be nurturing when the child is very young. Younger children need their parents for help more than teenagers. This dynamic may have yielded a sense of power in the narcissistic parent.

Good parents express love to teenagers in a different way than they do their young children. They offer interest, respect, support and boundaries as needed to their teenager. If the teenager feels safe enough they may not always show much appreciation for these offerings. Good parents do not take these moments too personally and remain available to their teenager. Love is not defined as doing for the teenager but in taking a step back and watching what the teenager can do for themselves.

This transition can be impossible for a domineering narcissistic parent. Their child may pick up on this. They may blame themselves for not being able to stay the way their parent can - seemingly - love them. If their parent grows cold, indifferent and contemptuous towards the adolescent this belief explains why. The adolescent then adult cannot expect anything from their parent because they are no longer loveable to that parent. The parent stays preserved as good in the person's mind.

"The world is a dangerous and untrustworthy place"

As kids grow they become more interested in the world outside of their family. They want to establish friendships and explore activities that bring them fulfillment. These healthy strivings would threaten the domineering narcissistic parent's fragile psychology.

The growing kid of such a parent may adopt this belief to thwart the actions that would threaten their parent. If the world is dangerous and people are untrustworthy then why leave home? Spoiling the growing kid's incentive to expand their worlds can leave the narcissistic parent free to keep domineering the kid. The kid is then spared the parent's attack and abandonment.

> *When he was fifteen, Ira felt a surge of self-loathing. He hated the way he looked. He thought he was terrible at the sports he played. He was disinterested in school. He would work at a local coffee shop after school some days. Life felt like a slog.*
>
> *All the while, Ira's home life felt like being under totalitarian rule. He relished the times before his father got home from work. Ira could lose himself in video games or movies. But when his father arrived Ira had to be on full alert. He would pay great attention to what*

his father said or found interesting. So long as he did this, his father would not attack him.

All the while, no adult showed interest or concern in Ira's own life. His internal tumult was completely hidden. The presence of adults felt threatening to him. He had to make himself small to placate them and hope that they would eventually leave him alone.

By his senior year in high school, Ira felt behind the other kids in his grade. They had been dating, getting involved in extracurricular activities, and having adventures with each other outside of school. Ira had withdrawn socially as he knew that his father would not let him enjoy a rich social life. It was easier to avoid relationships that his father would not let him participate in.

Ira was trying to prevent that dark future of growing up from happening at this stage. He had to sacrifice an incredible amount of what he was entitled to. Friendships, intimacy, prowess in activities he cared about. These things were implicitly forbidden under his father's watch.

Recovery involves picking up your adult self from storage

The spirit of scapegoat survivors never ceases to amaze me. Despite having been met with cruelty where they hoped to find love they maintain a drive to find and live the quality of life they deserve. Being the adult they are and feeling deserving of love for being that person was always the mission. It may get delayed but not denied.

In my therapeutic work with survivors much of it centers around knowing it is safe to be their adult selves. It was not safe to be openly mature when they were younger. Nothing can change that tragedy. What can be healed is a survivor's right to be who they are now - developmentally speaking - in their lives.

Being an adult in this sense means being entitled to the same amount of respect, goodwill and dignity as any other adult. It also means that no adult's well-being is more important than any other's. Nor is any one adult's opinion or thoughts worth more or less than any other adult's.

Finding it safe to be this kind of adult is to encounter continued care and support when being this way. The scapegoat survivor has had to learn that being fully upright is dangerous. That used to blow up their narcissistic parent's willingness to be their parent. What seemed like kindness was the parent's gratification at feeling more powerful than the child. The scapegoat survivor may gradually find it safe to expect love without sacrificing their power. Here the other person really wants you to feel as empowered and good about yourself as possible. Compared to what was known with the narcissistic parent it is far more about you.

Recovery through therapy

This kind of genuine concern for you can feel extremely unfamiliar at first. Scapegoat survivors may even have a hard time feeling it. What has been unsatisfying and hurtful has also been the most familiar in close relationships. What feels good and satisfying is new and takes repetition to make this feel real. Therapy can offer such repetition. Clients get to see over time that the two beliefs they had to adopt earlier do not have to apply in this setting.

Ira came to therapy in his late twenties. He was a successful professional but felt very isolated and anxious when he was not at work. He could think through the problems he had to solve when working alone. In larger meetings, however, he found it difficult to hold onto his own thoughts. He felt overwhelmed, small and resentful in these situations. As though what he had to say was not worthy of others' respect.

In privacy, Ira had a chance of feeling like his ideas and opinions mattered. But when he had an audience that seemed impossible. He felt like what he had to say was faulty and going to be regarded as stupid or inconsequential.

One of Ira's stated goals at the start of treatment was to have more confidence speaking up in his life. I worked to understand Ira's traumatic experiences at the hands of his father. Between this understanding and my experience of Ira in session, I inferred that he survived his domineering father by limiting the scope of his life. I suspected that Ira had to believe the world was dangerous and untrustworthy. I also wondered if Ira believed he deserved rejection if he took his place as a grown up in the world.

Treatment lasted for several years. It took time in this new therapeutic relationship for Ira to feel safe enough to begin testing these beliefs. Ira had always been interested in psychology. He was well-read on the impact of childhood maltreatment and psychological suffering. In the third year of treatment this session occurred.

Ira told me, "I was reading about trauma over the weekend and wondered something. It seems like my experience in meetings starts in my body. Like I "know" I'm nobody to be listened to before I even think about it. This book I was reading said that trauma gets stored in the body. I'm probably not analyzing it right. But I wondered what you think about it? I'm definitely not the expert here."

I paused. A lot seemed to be going on in this moment. Ira had a good and cogent insight into his experience. However he was packaging it to me almost as an apology. As if he might risk offending me by presuming to know more. I felt fairly certain that this was not a reflection of my attitude and behavior towards Ira. I regarded Ira as a very competent, strong, dignified, compassionate and earnest person. Maybe Ira was trying to test his belief that he deserved rejection if he took his place amongst grown-ups. Ira may have seen psychological insight as my sole dominion. By bringing up his own insights, Ira was presenting me with an opportunity to respond in a way that disconfirmed his belief.

I said, "You came up with a formidable insight about your current and past experience. And I was struck by your emphasis on me being the expert here. As though your contributions to this work are less valuable. Does that resonate with you at all?"

Ira said, "Well yeah. I actually feel this searing fear right now. Like I'm coming into your territory and trying to show you up. What right do I have to think I know something that you spend your whole career studying?"

Me: "Right. You have known such expressions of your own competence to be extremely dangerous in the past. What sort of reaction from me might be most harmful?"

Ira: "Well, you could think I'm some kind of jerk for trying to put you down. Then you would have to put me in my place and that would mean a lot of humiliation for me. Plus, it would feel like our relationship is gone forever."

Me: "Those would be devastating consequences."

Ira: "Yeah...well, that is what it feels like right now. But when I really think about it, I'm not trying to offend *you. I'm trying to help myself here and bring in something that is important."*

Me: *"Yes you are."*

Ira: *"So why should you actually try to destroy me for that? That used to happen all the time with my father, sure. I guess there is a part of me - sure it's small - that thinks this may not apply to you."*

In this example, I did not respond to him as the one with the expert opinion that was most important. I inquired why Ira was diminishing the importance of his own opinion. This may have helped Ira feel safer to question the belief that he would be rejected if he expected respect from me. These kinds of interactions would happen over and over in the course of his therapy. Over time, he felt safer to know and express the value of his perspective and abilities.

12

When Scapegoats Escape Inward to Survive Narcissistic Abuse

> *Does it seem impossible for both people in a relationship to feel good?*
> *Do you feel bad when you stand up for yourself even though you know it is the right thing to do?*
> *Are you unsure whether you are right to hold others accountable for their treatment of you?*

You may have heard the saying that when you point a finger at someone else there are always three fingers pointing back at you. There's certainly wisdom in this for those who are over eager to blame others for their troubles. For someone who survived narcissistic abuse as the scapegoat, however, this saying and the concept it reflects may need to be overcome.

The scapegoat survivor has experienced the narcissistic parent and colluding family members to relentlessly point their fingers at the survivor. They would then be accused of heresy if they dared to point a finger back in the family's direction. The result for the survivor can be a crippling of their reflex to fight back or protest when insulted

It is a two-pronged process of change from this dynamic of self-crippling as a way to feel close to someone. The goal is to be able to feel close to others while feeling fully possessed of yourself. It is a long road from the former to the latter, but a very worthwhile one.

When there's nobody to consistently connect to

A child needs a caregiving adult who is consistently good to that child. I don't mean perfectly good. In fact, infant-parent researchers have found that the most securely attached infant-parent bonds happen when the parent attunes to the infant about 30% of the time (Tronick & Gianino, 1986). This leaves a lot of room for missing each other and space for each party to attend to themselves. What is critical is that there is an ongoing motivation and intent to be available to the infant by the parent. When this is in place then the child gets to find a person outside of themselves upon whom they can depend, rely, and ultimately trust. By finding the source of what they need outside of themselves there gets to be a sense of continuity with who others are to the child and who the child is to themselves.

When a child does not get this – as is the case for those born to a pathologically narcissistic parent – then they have to turn inward to find the connection they seek. The child does not have a source outside of themselves consistent enough to count on. A narcissistic parent's self-absorption will prevent them from being truly available to the child. The child cannot be an ongoing priority to a narcissistic parent even at the 33% threshold.

A narcissistic parent may take grave offense at the child not smiling back when the parent smiles at them and decide to put that child down and leave the room. Or that same parent may want to stay on the phone with an adult friend because the parent's status feels boosted and ignore the child's pleas for attention. In these cases, the child learns that the parent's availability is highly volatile and can be directed towards others more than the child. The child does not have a person outside of themselves upon whom they can count, depend, and trust.

Now the child has to turn from their painful external reality towards an inner realm where they are freer to construct a world that is more friendly to them. This inner realm protects the child from the pain of the narcissistic parent's unavailability. It contains representation of the narcissistic parent the way the child wishes the parent was rather than how the parent actually is. The inner realm requires delicate treatment of everyone in it to maintain the fragile harmony the child needs. The function of this realm is to provide the child with a place they can get their needs met without requiring anything more from narcissistic parent in external reality.

As is so often the case when a child is abused or neglected, this solution creates new problems. Since the internal relationship to the wished-for parent is not real, it is very fragile. As the external narcissistic parent goes on being devaluing, depriving and controlling the scapegoat seeks to make these encounters be over with as fast as possible. The child wants to go back to their inner world where they feel less under siege. However, a new problem is created because now the child cannot intervene effectively with what is going on outside of themselves. Their entire being screams to get back to their inner world when the external party starts being a problem. The child's own reactions of anger at this mistreatment have to get short-circuited because they could draw the child further out into the external world with the narcissistic parent.

The child might short-circuit their own anger is to blame themselves when they get angry at the narcissistic parent. This can happen in the blink of an eye. The child may simultaneously hate themselves while hating the parent in that moment for being unavailable or attacking. The child is very much pointing three fingers back at themselves when trying to point one at the parent. Doing so makes the whole endeavor of getting and showing anger towards the parent too fraught internally and externally to proceed with.

From the outside it can look like the scapegoat child is surrendering to the parent or backing down from a fight. But this is not the case from the standpoint of the child's inner world. The child wants to get back to a realm where their internal others make sense, and things feel way less impossible. They have tragically learned that nothing good happens in the external world with someone else. It is best to go inward where things feel less unfixable. The parent gets to have their way while the scapegoat child has a way to ignore what is going on outside of them.

How does this affect the scapegoat survivor as an adult?

But, from where life gets lived –the scapegoat survivor's consciousness – the legacy of having to go into one's internal world to avoid danger rather than mix in with the external world can leave that person feeling foundationless when conflict arises. In this case, the survivor may do whatever they can – as they did with their narcissistic parent – earlier in life to make such conflictual situations subside.

What can be done?

If you had to burrow into your internal reality to save yourself from an external reality with a narcissistic parent, then new safe relationships will likely play an important role in making and finding allies in the external world today. The goal is to have a balanced mix of internal and external worlds.

To recover, a survivor can try to find and cultivate relationships with people who offer safety. Instead of asking whether they are acceptable to others, the survivor asks whether the others are acceptable. Evaluating the character of other people is something that is often unfamiliar for the scapegoat survivor but can make venturing back into the external world a much safer endeavor than it used to be. Making this shift in perspective allows the scapegoat survivor to populate their external world with actual people who treat the survivor well.

13

When Scapegoat Survivors Think: "It's Only Me Finds Who this Difficult"

> *When you feel challenged by a task do you also feel like you are the only who finds it challenging?*
> *Does feeling challenged remind you that you are inadequate in some way?*
> *When you look around does it seem like others can easily do what you are struggling to do?*

Most children are encouraged and supported when they encounter challenges in life. The scapegoat child to a narcissistic parent is not. If they encounter a challenge they are undermined or ignored. Neither reaction by the narcissistic parent sets the child up for success.

As a result, scapegoat children and survivors may avoid challenges. The emotional cost can be too severe. They have been conditioned to associate challenges with feeling inferior, strange and alone.

The problem is that challenges are a natural part of realizing our full potentials. To avoid them is to avoid one's full self. Scapegoat survivors are often painfully aware of this fact. They can experience a gnawing sense of not living as fully as they want to be. Yet the pain and felt futility of facing a challenge is too much.

One of the ways challenges can feel painful is in the experience that you are the only one facing them. The scapegoat child can believe they are inferior, strange and alone if something does not come easily. These conclusions weaken when they see that someone they admire faces similar struggles.

Challenges make the scapegoat child feel inferior, strange & alone

The scapegoat child is forced to believe they cannot do anything important right. The rub is that anything important is going to contain some challenging moments. Most people are encouraged to work to overcome challenges. When the scapegoat child encounters a challenge they go unsupported. Their parent may use the fact that the child is feeling challenged as proof that they are inferior. An adequate person - supposedly - would not find the situation challenging at all. This leaves the child and later the survivor feeling inferior, strange and alone when they take on challenges.

How the scapegoat child is made to feel <u>inferior</u> in the face of challenges

The scapegoat child is in a terrible predicament when it comes to their own self-worth. Their narcissistic parent does not want them to feel good about who they are and what they can do. This would threaten their ability to relocate their own worthlessness into the child. And yet, the child needs to retain hope that they can figure out how to one day be of worth.

Scapegoat children may stay hopeful that they have worth by privately telling themselves they are great. In this secret place within themselves they can insist on their worth. However, this worth has to be based on exaggerated claims about their traits and abilities. These claims are inflated to counter the parent's message that they are worthless.

The child cannot bring these elevated claims into their reality. Every time they do they come up short and feel crestfallen. The child who secretly sees themselves as the smartest person in their class is crushed by getting a 'B' grade. The child who sees themselves as the best soccer player is devastated when they do not make an all-star team. These setbacks are so painful because their parent is setting them up to feel worthless. A setback dunks the child in the tank of worthlessness that they are working so hard to save themselves from.

Over time the scapegoat child may avoid challenges. Experience tells them that the only result is feeling inferior. They cannot see how life has been rigged against them. They assume that their privately held high standards are their own and they are not living up to them.

Rick rarely felt loved as a child. For as long as he can remember he felt like a burden and an outcast to his family. His mother related to Rick as if he did not know the proper way to live. If he was walking in front of her she would say he was slouching and needs better posture. If he was chewing at the dinner table she would say he swallows his bites too soon and needs to slow down. If he was happy for any reason she would criticize him for being selfish.

Despite all of his mother's efforts to tear him down, Rick found a way to keep thinking of himself as likeable and smart. He would identify which of his classmates he wanted to become friends with. Then he would set about talking to them and playing with them at recess. Over time a friendship would develop.

In third grade, Rick saw that some of the kids got taken to a special class during the afternoons. He asked his teacher why and she told him that they were part of the gifted program. He resolved right there to gain access to it. He found out about the test he had to take and asked his teacher to recommend it for him. He took it and was told that he had done well enough to join the program. He was elated. He felt like now he could finally believe that there was something special about him.

His parents had to sign a permission slip to let him join. When his mother looked at it she unilaterally decided that he should not be separated from his other classmates. Rick's heart was broken. He begged and pleaded for her to change her mind to no avail. Rick spent the rest of third grade feeling the sting of inferiority every time his classmates were gathered to attend the gifted class.

Having a private elevated picture of yourself does not necessarily make you narcissistic. You can do this while still having empathy for others. It also does not mean that you coerce others to reflect back this elevated picture. It may just be something to be addressed in the recovery process. Finding a better quality of life requires a realistic basis for self-esteem.

Why the scapegoat child is made to feel <u>strange</u> in the face of challenges

Scapegoat children were often reacted to as if there was something uniquely wrong with them when they faced a challenge. To remark about the difficulty of something was to invite alienation. What is it about you, child, that you cannot easily do this? Their narcissistic parent pushes their own self-doubt into the child then recoils from it. The child is left feeling strange for finding a challenge to be difficult.

> *Jack was told to do a lot in his home growing up. Many of his father's demands were beyond what a kid Jack's age should be able to do. At age six, his father told him to clean the garage and that it should take him at least three hours. Jack felt a surge of frustration and despair charge through him. "But, Dad, I don't want to! It's Saturday. I want to go play with my friends."*
> *His Dad responded, "Oh, Mr. Whiner. What is it now?" as he derisively laughed at Jack.*

Jack felt the burn of shame added to his exasperation. His father was acting like it was a sign of weakness that Jack did not want to clean the garage. His complete lack of validation for Jack's protest left Jack feeling strange for finding this task daunting.

Jack was not strange for not wanting to clean a garage instead of play with his friends at age six. If his father had validated Jack's complaints, even if he continued to ask him to clean the garage, Jack would have felt less strange. But his father used this opportunity to mock Jack for complaining. His mockery likely served to protect himself from feeling daunted by any of his own tasks in life. It was his son, not he, who found certain tasks challenging. The threat to his inflated sense of self-worth had been nullified at Jack's great expense.

How the scapegoat child is made to feel <u>alone</u> in the face of challenges

The scapegoat child does not get the support and encouragement needed to find challenges attainable. Narcissistic parents see their own needs as most important. So if their child needs something from them then that child is "selfishly" taking away from who is most important. This logic extends to the child who seeks help and support in the face of a challenge.

The result for the child is going without the experience of available help in the face of challenges. The scapegoat child who faced a challenge would look around and find nobody on their side to shore up their belief in themselves.

Rick wanted to be the fastest runner on his cross-country team in high school. At the first practice he was beat handily by three of the other runners on the team. He felt dejected. "I'm nowhere near as good as I thought. I don't know what I was thinking."

He told no one of his disappointment because he expected them to react as if he was stupid in the first place for thinking he could be the fastest. He had to tend to this wound alone. He found his joy in running to wither over the course of the season. His goal was no longer to be the best but to not come in last.

A strategy to feel adequate, normal and connected in the face of challenges

I find writing to be important. As important as I find this process to be, it is not easy. Some days, when I sit down to write, my thoughts are running around like cats. Instead of seeing the progress made in what has been written so far, I might only see the flaws in it. A lot of the time I can find some footing to proceed with the writing. Sometimes, however, I just have to put it off for the day.

I've always felt inferior, strange and alone when these writing challenges come up. In my mind's eye I see the other people who write in this field and assume they face no such challenges. They sit down at their computer and produce 1500 impeccable words with ease.

This shifted the other day. I was talking to a trusted friend and colleague who also writes. I have always admired their writing and put them in the camp of finding it easy at all times. That day I could not get underway with the writing. I was frustrated. It occurred to me to ask my friend if he ever encountered challenges when trying to write. I wholly expected him to look at me like I was strange and exclaim that he never has. Instead, he surprised me.

He said, "Well, yeah. I procrastinate all the time. And then I get frustrated with myself for not writing as much as I had hoped that day."

I said, "Really? Do you ever find that you can't gather your thoughts or make a linear argument?"

He said, "Oh, absolutely. Other times I'll have so many different thoughts racing through that I can't seem to organize them."

I said, "I always thought I was the only one who found writing to be hard."

He said, "No way. You are not alone. It is not easy."

I bring up this story to illustrate one way to combat feeling inferior, strange and alone in the face of a challenge. Asking someone whom you admire and who is likely to be honest whether they find something challenging can counter the messages received about challenges from a narcissistic parent.

Benefits to asking others what they find challenging

Asking someone you admire whether they feel challenged in similar ways can help you conclude that you are not the only one. If someone you admire struggles at times, too, then you must not be inferior for doing the same.

These kinds of questions may help you discover you are on a more equal playing field with those you admire. A narcissistic parent goes out of their way to make their scapegoat child feel they are of lower status. Finding out that you are more similar than different to someone you admire when it comes to challenges can help restore your sense of equal status.

If you are in good company when challenged then there is less justification to criticize yourself. The scapegoat survivor gets to recalibrate their definition of what is 'good enough.' It no longer has to mean that everything comes easily.

Finally, you can find it safe to regard challenges as a normal part of pursuing important goals. The person you admire is able to achieve important goals. Yet they face similar challenges as you on the way to those goals. Challenges may therefore be expected in pursuit of anything meaningful. Instead of cause for self-criticism they can be signals that you are on a path that matters to you.

An exercise to de-stigmatize feeling challenged

This exercise will help you get firsthand information about whether you should feel inferior, alone and strange for facing challenges at times. Here are the steps:
1. Write down three goals that are important to you.
2. Write down all the challenges you face in reaching these goals.
3. Select someone you admire who is pursuing or has achieved this goal.
4. Find a way to ask that person if they face or have faced similar challenges.
5. Record the results.

Whenever you feel challenged and self-critical you can refer to this document. Over time you may feel much less stigmatized for feeling challenged.

14

Four Reasons the Scapegoat Child is Stronger Than Their Narcissistic Parent

> *Have you heard that the scapegoat child is often the healthiest member of the narcissistic family but never known why?*
> *Do you find this idea hard to believe?*
> *Do you wonder how someone can be strong while feeling weak?*

To those who know scapegoat survivors and the narcissistic parent they survived, it is clear that the survivor is psychologically stronger than the parent. This is often news to the scapegoated person. They have had to get used to seeing themselves as deficient and defective in relation to their parent. When, for example, a therapist tells the survivor that they were, in fact, stronger, it can seem like hearing something they have secretly known all their lives. At the same time they may be skeptical of it. How could I have been stronger", they may ask, "if I had to tip-toe around a parent who was calling all the shots?". In this case the definition of strength is something one can possess even while feeling weak.

I recently saw this form of strength is in the book and TV series the Handmaid's Tale. It is a story of a dystopian religious state where women's fertility rates have plummeted. Those women who are capable of bearing children - called handmaids - are forced to become slaves of ruling-class families where they must conceive and bear the husband's children under the watch of the wife. The main character is a handmaid named June who lives with a family where the wife immediately hates her for being able to bear children while she cannot. The wife goes out of her way to devalue and control June. If we understand this wife as being pathologically narcissistic then she uses June as her scapegoat. Yet, to anyone who has watched the show or read the book it is apparent that June is psychologically stronger than the wife. She was not stronger because she prevented the wife from abusing her. She demonstrated her strength in how she found a way to survive the abuse.

Being more powerful does not equal strength

A narcissistic parent often needs the scapegoat child to feel weaker than them. If the parent feels a core sense of weakness then inducing weakness in the child can relocate this troublesome feeling. By seeing the scapegoat child as the weak one, the parent feels buffered from this experience. To do this they devalue, deprive and control the child.

The scapegoat child only knows a life where their choices are not their own. They are left in a world of fear and undeservedness. They are coerced to feel less than the narcissistic parent and do.

The child in this position would be in disbelief if you told them that they were actually stronger than their parent. It is hard to believe you are stronger than the person who has a boot on your figurative neck. Here is why it is in fact true:

Just because someone is in a position of power over another does not make them stronger. A narcissistic parent is in a position of power over their scapegoat child by sheer fortune. They have not won this position by merit. They simply gave birth to a child who needs them more than they need that child. As such, it is entirely possible for the person in power to be psychologically weaker than the child. In fact, their weakness may get expressed by exerting power over their child.

If psychological strength does not equal power over others then what does it mean? Here are four traits that reflect true psychological strength. I see these traits show up time and again in my clinical work with scapegoat survivors. These traits seemed to help them endure the pain of childhood and find ways to heal from it.

Strength #1: Flexibility

The scapegoat child is inherently flexible. They can take others' perspectives. If the demands of situation call for it, they can also go along with the other's perspective.

This trait is required to stay in the narcissistic parent's reality. The narcissistic parent's perspective is distorted by their need to deny their own feelings of low self-worth. The scapegoat child has to psychologically stretch themselves to live in the parent's perspective.

Flexibility often gets mistaken for not having a backbone. Scapegoat survivors may criticize themselves for supposedly "bending to the narcissistic parent's will". This view does not include the fact that survival meant finding a way to share in the parent's reality. Their psychological flexibility allowed them to do this.

And not everyone possesses such flexibility. The narcissistic parent, for example, demonstrates extreme rigidity in their perspective. They must guard their inflated yet fragile self-worth so that they can only hold perspectives that conform.

A scapegoat child learns that the narcissistic parent will take everything personally. Whatever happens around the parent will be seen as a referendum on the parent's worthiness. The narcissistic parent is unable to consider other perspectives. Their psychology has formed too rigidly to defend themselves from threatening information.

John found himself able to relate to a wide variety of people. In high school he worked at a car wash with coworkers who were 20 years older. On his basketball team he got along with his teammates. He found ways to connect with his teachers. It seemed easy to him to pay attention to someone and figure out where they were coming from. He could meet them where they figuratively stood with little effort.

> John also had a wrathful narcissistic father who cast all of John's traits in a negative light. When John got home from work and was sharing a good experience he had with his coworkers, his father's response was often something like: "Boy, you know just what to say to get people to like you, don't you? I bet they don't even realize what you're doing to them."
>
> John felt a surge of shame as he suddenly found himself feeling like a bad and manipulative guy. His father must be seeing something that was plain as day. John could not even trust himself to realize how 'bad and deceitful' he was.

In this example, John's strength of flexibility seemed to threaten his narcissistic father. To nullify the threat, his father distorted John's strength into a supposed character defect.

Strength #2: Emotional maturity

The scapegoat child demonstrates significantly more emotional maturity than the narcissistic parent. They are informed by, not dominated by, their emotions. They can do this because of their unusually high capacity to introspect.

The scapegoat child is on their own to navigate their feelings. The narcissistic parent casts this child as an adversary to them and the family. This leaves them without someone to express and regulate their strong emotions with.

The scapegoat survivors that I have had the privilege to work with are phenomenally introspective and use this to manage their feelings on their own. The scapegoat child may be endowed with an unusually high capacity for introspection. Introspection - or looking within - requires the ability to be curious about what one is feeling. The child who engages in introspection is trying to figure out what their feelings and others' feelings mean in the current context. They take their feelings as suggestions rather than facts about what is going on around them.

It is probably obvious that a narcissistic parent is emotionally immature. They are dominated by their emotions. They see their feelings as facts and navigate the world accordingly. For example, let us say that the scapegoat child demonstrates an ability that the parent covets which leads to the parent feeling envy-based shame. The parent feels pain in relation to this child therefore the child must be bad. They do not have the capacity to introspect and wonder why they feel such intense shame in observing their child's abilities.

> *John mostly kept a level head in his life. When his friends lost their temper on the basketball court he was the one who would step in and get them to calm down. He was selected by his school counselor to be part of a student leadership committee.*
>
> *His father could not stand to see John's emotional stability. Whenever he was in a full rage and John was speaking to him calmly he grew even more furious. He*

hated that John was in control of himself, and he was not. He would take away John's freedoms until he got to one that John really cared about. At that point, John would pound his fist on the counter or sink to his knees in despair. Then his father would exclaim, "Look who's throwing a tantrum!".

John possessed a great deal of emotional maturity. However his father's efforts to flood John with despair then accuse him of being immature confused him. He wondered how he could be so calm and collected at school but have such "tantrums" at home. It could not occur to him at the time that his father was goading him. John had to conclude that he was really the emotionally immature person his father claimed he was and his calmness at school was just an act.

Strength #3: Driven towards the truth

The truth matters a great deal to the scapegoat child and survivor. Though they have had to go along with their parent's distorted reality they are bothered at a deep level that it is not true. The scapegoat child's psychology is oriented to knowing what is real. They are bothered by living in denial.

During childhood, survival demands they suppress their need to know what is true. Once enough distance has been obtained from their narcissistically abusive parent, they can safely seek the truth. This means prizing accurate information regardless of how it makes one feel. Knowing what is true scratches a fundamental itch for the scapegoat survivor.

I see this propensity towards the truth every day in my practice. Scapegoat survivors are motivated to come to therapy to be able to live in unison with the truth. They have been pained by having to live at odds with it to keep their narcissistic parent gratified.

The truth they have survived is too overwhelming to know on their own. To paraphrase an important psychoanalytic theorist, named Wilfred Bion: we cannot think some thoughts without another person. The thought that a parent cannot offer the love that was needed fits this category for the scapegoat child. Therapy affords the other person needed to think and know what happened. The reward is they get to satisfy their drive to know the truth. The drive towards truth may explain why scapegoat survivors come to therapy so much more than pathological narcissists.

In contrast to the scapegoat survivor, the narcissistic parent can live in denial of who they actually are and what they actually did in the scapegoat survivor's childhood. They may be incapable of tolerating the shame they would feel if they sought the truth. They prioritize feeling good over knowing reality. They do not possess the psychological strength to do otherwise.

John sought therapy in his mid-twenties and began to tell me about his upbringing. I told him that his father's behavior was abusive. This confirmed something John always knew. He thought back to all the times he would argue with his father that he was being unfair to John to no avail.

After six months of therapy John returned home for a holiday. He was brimming with excitement to tell his father how devalued he felt as his son. He was ready to recount his father's abusive treatment and expected to be met with a sincere apology. Instead he was shocked that his father flatly denied all of John's memories. He told him: "Boy, you really know how to bend the truth to your advantage, don't you? Get out of here with these lies, John. I raised you right and if you think different then that's your problem not mine."

John's concern with setting the record straight about the past with his father reflected his drive towards the truth. His father showed his willingness to deny the truth to avoid feeling bad by dismissing John's claims.

Strength #4: Empathy

The scapegoat child can perceive and care about the feelings of others. This is so despite receiving very little of the same from their narcissistic parent.

Similar to flexibility, a scapegoat survivor may wonder why empathy is a strength. They may see their empathy for the narcissistic parent as what led to being exploited. I think this view loses sight of the fact that the child's survival depended on meeting the narcissistic parent's emotional demands. The scapegoat child who could empathically understand their narcissistic parent's vulnerability to feeling worthless stood a better chance at surviving. This understanding allowed the child to avoid actions perceived as offensive by their parent.

Outside of the context of the narcissistic parent empathy is also a strength. Being able to attune to and care about someone else's feelings leads to healthy relationships. Healthy people are drawn to being understood and having their feelings matter to someone else. The scapegoat child and survivor's capacity for this often leads to being quite popular outside the family.

The narcissistic parent is bereft of this strength. Their lack of empathy may be what makes it possible to abuse their child without concern for the child's wellbeing. They navigate life by seeing who can add to their exaggerated self-worth. There is a glaring incapacity to care about the inner worlds of those others. As a result, pathologically narcissistic people are unable to sustain reciprocal relationships. This can lead to a pattern of broken and/or unsatisfying relationships.

> *John was acutely aware of his father's feelings in any given moment. He could predict what types of circumstances would lead to his father feeling slighted and therefore hostile. He would use his empathic awareness of his father's feelings to try to prevent explosions of rage as much as he could.*

For example, John knew that his father would feel like he did not matter if John asked for permission to join his friends at a party. So, John would be sure to tell his father how much he appreciated him in the days leading up to the party. Then on the day of, John would nonchalantly say that someone had invited him to a party and he did not really want to go but he did not want to disappoint his friend. Then he would ask his father what he thought. Often his father might say, "Go to the party, what do I care?".

John employed his empathy to keep himself as safe as possible from his father's temper and find a way to get moments of freedom where possible. He bought himself experiences of socialization that were so important for his development. Knowing he had a way to get his father's permission to see his friends also gave him hope that sustained him through his adolescence.

Once John had moved away from his family he was surprised to find how empathic people found him. His girlfriend, at one point, told him that she really appreciates how he listens to her and easily understands how she is feeling. John expected her to see this as something he was "up to" or that he was "just saying the right thing" like his Dad would accuse him of. But she meant this in a wholly sincere way.

As John continued in therapy, he saw how his ability to empathize with others was highly valued by them.

Give yourself the credit you are due

There is a particularly unfair aspect to the narcissistic parent's treatment of the scapegoat child. The parent is only able to offload their own sense of worthlessness onto the child because the child is psychologically strong enough to bear it. So, the parent profits from the child's strength but will not credit the child in any way.

This is exquisitely unfair to the scapegoat child because such credit might give them something they could rightfully value in themselves. They could see and know themselves as psychologically strong.

As unfair as the omission of credit for your strength was in childhood it is not too late to grant it to yourself. I think that this can be one of the important outcomes from therapy. By working with someone who can see your strengths they get to be something you know exists in the world.

15

Self-Consciousness in Scapegoat Survivors of Narcissistic Abuse

> *Do you worry that something about you makes you stand out in a bad way?*
> *Do you find it hard to live without thinking there is some sort of problem with you?*
> *Do you worry that the more someone gets to know you the less they will like you?*

It is no accident that scapegoat children of narcissistic parents often feel self-conscious. These children have to embody the worthlessness their parent cannot tolerate in themselves. Having to perceive oneself as objectionable makes a person conscious of who they are. They have to worry that others will "see" how defective they supposedly are. It becomes extremely hard to forget oneself and assume acceptance from others.

When a parent calls attention to the child's habits, posture, speech, gait, manners, weight, temperament, elocution and/or intelligence the child can feel like an object to the parent. Being an object to the person you depend on is an awful experience. You have no say in how they see you based on your definition of yourself. Instead you have to become conscious of and operate within their definition of you. For the scapegoat child the parent's definition of them is biased by the parent's need to see the child as "less than". So the child is trapped in the parent's gaze of them and that gaze is rigged to make the child feel different, disgusting, and devalued.

A narcissistic parent's scrutiny can make a scapegoat child self-conscious. The parent may scrutinize aspects of the child that are real but distort them into qualities to feel ashamed of. For example, a narcissistic parent who is insecure about their own intelligence may tease an intelligent child for being such an "egghead." Now, the child's good quality feels like a reason for embarrassment. This child becomes conscious of a self that is preoccupying, shameful and alien. The way out for scapegoat survivors is a new relationship where they feel understood and accepted from the inside out.

Why a narcissistic parent makes a scapegoat child feel self-conscious

The parent has to make up reasons to see their scapegoat child as lower status. These reasons then become prophecies the child has to live out. One of the ways a parent can convince their child of their lower status is by scrutinizing them. Instead of seeing the child's existence as fundamentally understandable and normal, the parent calls it into question. The pay attention to the child under the auspices of "noticing" what is strange about the child. Scapegoat children are often familiar with the dread of hearing their name in the narcissistic parent's mouth. This often involved the parent talking about their child in subtly humiliating ways.

> Devin was big for his age as a first-grader. He liked to rough house with his friends and was infatuated with being strong. He would watch the movie Hercules repeatedly because he was delighted by it.
>
> One day he went shopping for clothes with his pathologically narcissistic mother. She looked at him and said, "Devin, you're husky. We need to find clothes that will fit a husky boy." Devin wasn't sure what this meant. "Mom, what does husky mean?". She said, "It means that you have bigger bones than other kids your age."
>
> He went to try on clothes and she frowned and said "Your waist is too big for these pants. I'll go get a bigger size." He was confused. He felt like she saw something wrong with his body but couldn't say exactly what.
>
> The next week they were visiting his maternal grandparents and his mother said at the dinner table: "Devin is big for his age. I took him clothes shopping last week and we had to go to the Husky section." Devin felt embarrassed but he still wasn't exactly sure why. He wondered why his mother was making such a big deal out of him being big for boys his age. He overheard her on the phone telling other parents about his husky clothes. He felt singled out and put down.

At the dinner table she would point out that Devin did not chew his food enough and ate too fast. She said that was why he was too big. Devin felt terrible. Now he knew there must be something wrong with his body.

At around this time, Devin stopped seeing himself as a strong boy and started seeing himself as disgustingly overweight. He saw this when he looked in the mirror and feared that his classmates thought the same of him. He grew extremely conscious of his body and couldn't shake the feeling that it was a liability instead of an asset.

What Devin did not know was that his mother was worried about her own weight at the time. She had been quite thin up until that point and seemed to feel threatened by having put on some weight. She transferred this fear of her own perceived defect onto her son by calling so much attention to his body. Although she did not directly state he was overweight, her harping on the subject was enough to make Devin self-conscious. Seeing him self-conscious about his body helped her disassociate from her own fears of being physically unappealing.

What life is like for the scapegoat child

The scapegoat child is in the vulnerable position of needing to be who their parent recognizes. If the parent sees them as strange then the child had better believe they are strange. To believe otherwise would risk diverging from the parent's reality. Better to be a defective somebody to someone than a nobody to no one.

The scapegoat child gets coerced into being the one who has something wrong with them. Just like Devin's mother kept bringing up his 'husky' body so the narcissistic parent keeps insisting on the child's defectiveness. The child cannot help but assume the parent is right to focus on their - supposed - defect.

Lastly, the narcissistic parent often finds some small basis in reality upon which to transfer their defective feelings. In Devin's case, it was that he was, in fact, big for his age. His mother used this fact to relocate her own weight insecurities onto him. Devin found her insinuations about him more believable because there was something about him that served as the hook for them to hang on.

Thus, the scapegoat child is forced into being self-conscious about one or more aspects of themselves. There are three features to this self-consciousness in the child's and later the survivor's experience.

Feature #1: Preoccupation

It takes a lot of work for the scapegoat child to stay self-conscious. This is because their natural being does not correspond to what they have to be self-conscious about. The child is not - in fact - what they are self-conscious about. But to be self-conscious they must harass themselves with these reminders of their - supposed - defectiveness.

The scapegoat child is in a predicament. They want relief from the agony of self-consciousness yet find it impossible to stop. To not be self-conscious in these ways would be to have no relationship to their parent. It is always better to be anxiously preoccupied about supposed defects in themselves and known to a parent than to go unknown.

Feature #2: Shameful

The scapegoat child's attention gets called to their supposed defect because of the alarm bell of shame. They have been supposedly shown how they "really are" by their narcissistic parent. This information was received in a way where the child was seen as a defective object. For this to happen, there has to be a break in the subject-to-subject connection that we all want ideally. To hope to be seen from the inside and instead be seen as a defective object is inherently shaming.

Such experience overwhelms the child's abilities to cope in the moment. After a trauma like this it can be natural to rehearse it. The child can feel like they need to stay aware of it to make sure it does not happen again. Or if it does that they can survive it this time. This means keeping the experience of shame in one's consciousness so that they are not ambushed again by it.

Feature #3: Alien

No matter how much the scapegoat child has to torture themselves via self-consciousness there is a nagging sense that none of it is true. This feature can be hard for the child to articulate at the time. Experientially, there can be a sense that the way their parent is treating them does not feel real. However, the child has to prioritize the parent's claim of what is real over their own. This means having to cling to an identity that feels ill-fitting yet necessary.

> *Devin now had to contend with the premise that he was objectionably overweight to himself and to others. It flooded his thoughts. He always felt on the verge of embarrassment for this. Shame was a constant and unwelcome companion in his world now.*

> *Devin felt lost if he wasn't thinking of what to do about his defect. He also felt an underlying bewilderment when he was thinking about his defect. It was as if he had a secret language that skewered him, and he could only speak with his mother. She spoke this language to him and he understood it by thinking himself in the way she led him to. Outside of this pathological arrangement, this identity did not hold. Devin had no other viable relationship with a caring adult to figure this out with. He was on his own in this respect. The only thing he could do was go along with his mother's ideas about who he was. This meant staying occupied with the shameful*

supposed fact that he was overweight and ignoring how alien this felt to him.

Devin functioned in his life on top of this bed of defectiveness. No matter what he did or accomplished it was marred by this underlying supposed reality. It became a wobbly fact of life that he had to keep with him at all times.

How to escape the binds of self-consciousness

Liberating oneself from this type of self-consciousness is a process. There are two challenges in doing this. First, being self-conscious to stay close to someone important may be what attachment feels like. If that is the case, then a different way of feeling attached is needed before the old way can be given up. Second, the pull to feel self-conscious may get reinforced by finding friends and partners who also require it. The scapegoat survivor may not feel close unless someone is shining a light on their supposed defect.

Therapy can help scapegoat survivors overcome these two challenges. First, a therapist has extremely low odds of needing their client to feel self-conscious so that they do not have to. So you can be sure that you will not be with someone who reinforces your self-consciousness. Second, a therapist's job is to facilitate understanding of how you have had to define closeness and whether that makes you happy or not. This can empower the scapegoat survivor to identify the forces that go into them feeling self-conscious. As they participate in the therapy and are free from those forces, they can make different choices. In order for this to happen, though, a sense of attachment needs to develop in therapy. This alternative form of attachment must be experienced for the survivor to give up the only form of attachment they know.

Devin sought therapy in his mid-twenties because he felt imprisoned by his anxious self-consciousness. He explained to me that he had found his appearance to be objectionable since he was young. Nothing we discussed seemed to change this in the first couple years of treatment. However, Devin consistently attended his sessions and he began to look forward to them as a place to relax and entertain whatever thoughts he had in the moment with me. He had not been afforded such a relationship growing up. People in his family could not communicate from a baseline sense of caring about one another. Interactions did not feel safe. Devin was beginning to experience what safety in a relationship felt like.

Over time Devin was able to make more use of my interpretation that his current self-consciousness was a way to stay close to his internalized narcissistic mother. He did not win an internal argument to "prove" that his appearance was acceptable. It was more like he turned away from that premise entirely. This was apparent in one particular session:

Devin said, "You know, I think I'm a healthy guy - psychologically and physically. It's kind of scary to say that, actually, but I think it's true."

I nodded and listened intently.

"I just had this image come to mind. It's like I was shanghai'd onto a boat where the captain and the crew told me there was something wrong with me. I walked around the ship and did my sailing chores thinking they were right."

"But now I feel like I have leaped off of that old boat and onto a boat that I'm steering and you are on board. On this boat I know I am healthy. I also know that you know I am healthy. It feels totally different but I'm still on a boat and going where I need to go."

This session demonstrates how Devin was able to give up the old way of thinking about himself in favor of what had developed between him and I.

16

How the Scapegoat Survivor May Confuse Badness with Realness

> *Do you define the 'real you' as someone who has low self-worth, is insecure, or anxious?*
> *Do your own good feelings seem inauthentic or superficial?*
> *Does life seem like it needs to be a struggle to feel real to you?*

The scapegoat child to a narcissistic parent is no stranger to feeling bad. If this form of abuse is chronic and severe enough the child can confuse badness with who they are. After surviving a childhood of narcissistic abuse, good feelings may feel inauthentic.

There are good reasons that the scapegoat survivor may feel this way. But the pursuit of an authentic "bad self," while compelling, can still be false. A scapegoat survivor can take steps to make a good self feel real.

How the scapegoat child is led to confuse badness with realness

All children depend on their primary caregivers to be a frame of reference for who they are. Parents are in a particularly powerful position to signal to the child what about them is real. The ways the child is responded to will tend to feel more real than what goes ignored.

In good-enough scenarios, the child's parents appreciate and respond to the child. They hold a baseline level of unconditional acceptance towards the child. Then they notice the original expressions, traits, and ways of the child. This gives the child a sense that they are understood how they understand themselves. There is a comfortable symmetry between the child's inner world and how the caregiver responds to that world. The child feels real for who they actually are in the world.

The scapegoat child's unique ways of being go unnoticed by their narcissistic parent. Instead the narcissistic parent sees this child as an instrument to get their own needs met. The child is earmarked to embody the worthlessness the parent cannot bear to feel.

The narcissistic parent cherry picks faulty attributes of the child to recognize. None of us are perfect. The scapegoat child - like all children - makes mistakes. The narcissistic parent selectively responds to these mistakes with scorn and contempt. This happens against a backdrop of not responding to the child's good traits. A scapegoat child is left to conclude that the only things real about them are bad.

> Greg was the scapegoat in his family of origin. His mother was narcissistic. She insisted on her perfection and found him to be the worthless one in the family. She would lash out in vindictive rage if she perceived even the slightest of criticisms or insults.
>
> His childhood was an ongoing gauntlet of her and his dad finding fault in him. They would go to church on Sundays and afterward have breakfast at a diner. At that time, eating was his only source of feeling good. Greg loved food and would eat with great relish.
>
> "Greg, chew your food before you swallow!," his mother would exclaim - bringing his father and sister's derisive attention towards him. On the car ride home she started a conversation about how Greg eats too fast with his father. "Greg just will not chew his food. He just swallows it down whole. He's going to become obese." Greg felt searing shame and intense worry that he was going to turn into something bad. He was not sure what 'obese' meant but he knew it was not good.
>
> Greg looked out the window to get absorbed in what he saw and leave these feelings behind. Something felt like it was inside his nose. Greg stuck his finger in to get it out. "Ew, he's picking his nose now!" exclaimed his sister. His mother spun around in her seat with unbridled contempt. "Greg get your hand out of your

nose right now, Darnit! You can't go around picking your nose like that. It's disgusting."

In the third grade Greg was winning his weekly class spelling bees on a regular basis. Greg lost in an early round one week because he spelled 'development' with an extra 'e'. As Greg came to the lunchtable to sit with his friends he said with full sincerity, "I'm really stupid". Saying that seemed like the truth. The feelings of dejection and disappointment in himself were what he felt so often at home. His friend, Sally, got up from the table and was so upset by what Greg said that she told his teacher. Greg did not know what to do with it then but knew he felt protected. Greg was in a family where everyone picked on him all the time, and now someone was saying that he should not pick on himself? That it pained them to see him hurt himself like this?

The only responses Greg tended to get from his parents were that he was defective. They ignored his strengths. Over time their continued emphasis on his mistakes led him to conclude that this was what was real about him. He assumed that when people saw and heard him that they recoiled in disgust like his mother. Of course, Sally, offered a powerful example to the contrary but Greg could not make use of it at that point in his life.

The siren song of catharsis for the scapegoat survivor

The scapegoat child is conditioned to feel real only when they feel bad about themselves. One way this can manifest as the child grows up is by searching for a way to wholly become this negative identity. Here is how and why this occurs.

The scapegoat child who is forced to think of themselves as bad also feels like something is amiss. There can be a lurking sense of not feeling entirely real and feeling incomplete. When this happens, the scapegoat survivor may seek to feel more complete by accessing and expressing how bad they feel about themselves. This, they have learned, is what is real about them. So ratcheting up these feelings should lead to feeling complete and authentic.

There can be a subtle hope that feeling one's badness will lead to a salvation of sorts. This hope may mimic the scapegoat child's understanding of why their narcissistic parent was so hostile. The child has to assume that the parent would not be so contemptuous if they were better. So if the child can take full ownership of their badness then maybe they can be forgiven by the parent and loved. It would be a salvation for the child in this predicament. Unfortunately, both forms of salvation are mirages.

The scapegoat survivor feels incomplete because the idea of their badness is inauthentic. The narcissistic parent's selective responses to their mistakes as a child were a fabrication. The intent was to get the child and the parent to believe the lie that the child was worthless. So, the child is going to feel a gnawing sense of being inauthentic because their identity is built on a lie.

> At Greg's first job after college he received his first performance review. Before walking into his boss's office he braced himself to be told how bad of an employee he was. As he sat down, he said, "Look, I want to come clean with you. I don't think I've done as a good a job as I can. I want to so please don't pull any punches in telling me how I can improve." Admitting his flaws at the outset felt honest to him.
>
> To his surprise his boss said, "Well, Greg you've given me no reason to throw any punches. You care about your work. You turn in good to excellent deliverables. If anything, I would want to address your perception of your performance. I think you are short-changing yourself."
>
> In a situation where Greg could be evaluated well or poorly his sense of badness initially tried to take control. He "confessed" his underperformance and openness to being shown how to improve. This felt like he was being honest about who he was - in the way his family had conditioned him to think of himself. His boss's response highlighted how Greg was actually received in his world. But at the time, Greg found this feedback to be confusing and unreal to him.

Finding what is good and real in yourself

The task for the scapegoat survivor is to redefine what is real about themselves. To date, real may have been the same as being flawed. Recovery involves resisting the siren song of doubling down on this identity. Next the survivor can try what feels unfamiliar or even unreal. This step may mean tolerating feelings of being lost, disoriented, inauthentic, and anxious.

I cannot overstate how important safe others are to this process. As the scapegoat survivor moves from the narcissistic family who responded to them as if they were bad they need responses from people who see the good in them. That is what will make goodness as a basis of their identity feel real in due time.

This process takes time because we are programmed to privilege our family's view of us. The scapegoat survivor has to surrender their allegiance to their family's view of them. This is hard by itself. Next, the survivor attempts to replace this view with safe friends' and partners' views of them. Although these views will be more accurate and kind, they will initially feel unfamiliar. The survivor may also feel disloyal for believing people outside their family. These feelings are all understandable and can be temporary. With persistence and time, these feelings can subside, and a new, more accurate definition of 'real' can take hold.

When Greg was in his mid-twenties he went to therapy. He knew he felt off inside but he didn't know why nor what to do about it. We started working together.

In the fourth year of treatment, Greg saw more clearly the ways he actually was in the world. He was funny. He was intelligent. He was warm and kind. He was drawn to woodworking. He was drawn to cooking. He also knew that when he did these things he felt unreal, anxious, and even depressed. It was the mutual understanding he had with me that helped him persist. He did not feel alone in trying to make real the actual parts of himself that had gone unresponded to by his narcissistic mother.

Greg committed to acting these ways in the world as much as he could. Sometimes, when he was going to woodworking class, it seemed like every part of him was screaming not to go. And yet, he would proceed. Over time, his inner resistance to doing what was good and real about him subsided. He now had a supportive relationship with me that helped him understand these feelings and push through them.

This process itself took several years. Progress was sure but incremental. At the end of treatment, Greg could say that he had a new frame of reference for who he was that was good and felt fairly real. The old frame of reference would still creep in at times but Greg could now see it as a familiar but false inner state.

17

When Getting Better Feels Like 'Selling Out' After Narcissistic Abuse

> *Does taking good care of yourself feel like a chore that you better do 'or else'?*
> *Do you feel bossed around internally to do what is expected?*
> *Do you feel 'lazy' or worse unless you are doing something meant to improve yourself?*

Sometimes a narcissistic parent takes a deceptive approach to abusing the scapegoat child. Instead of outright telling the child they are worthless, the parent attacks the child supposedly on the child's behalf. They claim the child does not know how to act "properly" and that these behaviors are going to get them "in trouble" in the outside world if they are not "corrected" by the parent.

The scapegoat child is in a vulnerable position because they need to bond to their parent. So the child will work to do or not do what the parent attacks them for. A narcissistic parent may attack the child for not doing things that are generally positive. They may rage at the child for not putting their plate in the sink after dinner. Or scream at the child for being 2 minutes late for dinner.

A child in a loving home is not scrutinized in such a manner. Foibles like being a couple minutes late or leaving the dinner table without putting the plate in the sink are not capital offenses. As a result, the child gets to come to their own conclusions about the importance of, say, being tidy or punctual.

The scapegoat child has to be tidy and punctual or face the narcissistic parent's rage. Whatever the child has to do to avoid their parent's wrath will also feel coerced. At some level, the child hates having to meet the narcissistic parent's unreasonable demands while having no say in the matter.

Later, the scapegoat survivor can feel like they are betraying themselves when they do today what they used to be forced to do. The trouble can be when those things are otherwise good to do. So, the survivor can find the expectation to be on time unbearably oppressive. Or the prospect of cleaning their home can feel enslaving. The survivor may try to stay loyal to themselves by not doing these things.

This sets the survivor up to later resent doing things that are otherwise good to do. They can feel like they are betraying themselves. Recovery eventually allows the survivor to see how they were betrayed by what their parents did to them, *not* by what they are doing to themselves.

Narcissistic abuse that is - supposedly - for your own good

One way a narcissistic parent asserts their superiority is attacking how the child takes care of themselves. The parent scrutinizes the child for the slightest mistake in table manners. In attitude and action they rail at the child for being so "lazy" or "sloven". They accuse the child of not brushing their teeth before bed. They infantilize their teenager by asking if they washed their hands after leaving the bathroom. They essentially treat the child as being incapable of caring for themselves. By extension, the parent is superior to the child for - supposedly - knowing better.

Limit the narcissistic parent's wrath by any means necessary

The child is in a no-win situation that they must survive. They already feel deprived of the basic respect, appreciation and love that all children need from a parent. This puts the child in an ongoing state of dis-ease within. Something essential is missing in their world but there is no help. Against this backdrop, the parent's contemptuous attack can feel unsurvivable. The child is already under-nourished and is now being attacked by whom they would expect nourishment.

To cope, the scapegoat child must find a way to limit their parent's hostility towards them. If the parent targets the child's inability to take care of themselves, then the child must find a way to do this. They command themselves to keep their elbows off the table at dinnertime, make their bed in the morning, and wash their hands. The child has to boss themselves around internally to not give the parent a reason to attack them. This gives the child hope of being spared their parent's scathing disapproval. Without this hope, the child would feel too anxiously vulnerable to function.

Somewhere within the child they register that they are being forced to do these things. Like all human beings, they take great offense at the denial of their basic human freedom. It is far too unsafe to voice this offense to the narcissistic parent. Only further attack or invalidation would occur. So, this well-founded resentment has to be made unconscious.

The child tries to make these conditions more palatable by convincing themselves their parent is right. Now, the parent is doing them a favor by criticizing them in these ways. They are giving the child a map for how to live properly that the child would otherwise be lost without.

> *Alexis's father was narcissistic and kept himself emotionally afloat by acting as if he knew and deserved better than her. He relentlessly found ways to pick on her. If she cleared her throat he would make a demonstration over how "disgusting" she was. If she was speaking to someone in public around him then he would later tell her she mumbles. If she got dressed for school he would often tell her to go change her clothes*

because they didn't match. If they were eating a meal he would tell her that she eats too fast and is going to get fat that way. He would tell the same story about her not taking a shower for a week when she was twelve over and over. He would criticize her posture if she was just standing still. "Alexis you have terrible posture. Stand up straight." He would always accuse her of having a messy room and say she could not see her friends until she cleaned it to his satisfaction. He was rarely satisfied. Her father curated an image of Alexis as a sloven, messy, gluttonous and unclean kid. He got to seem like the paragon of organization, maturity, discipline and cleanliness in contrast to her.

Alexis was confused by his treatment. She knew she was smart. She got decent grades at school. So why couldn't she do things that seemed so basic? She could not entertain at the time that she had a father who was propping himself up at her expense. Instead, she had to assume that she was stupid and prone to laziness. Her father was doing her the favor of correcting these bad qualities for her. She grew wary of her own judgment because she anticipated that he would "show" her how poor it was.

The only hope she had to limit his wrath in these ways was to make a show of how she was following his "rules." If he saw her going out of her way to spend hours cleaning her room, he would still feel the superiority he needed but would not have to berate her to get it. The same went for her forcing herself to have good posture *and asking him to evaluate it, or eating very slowly and making sure he noticed.*

Internally, Alexis felt pushed around by this coping strategy. She had to command herself to take these measures. If she balked, then she risked her father's degrading attacks all over again. She would often feel like a "sell-out" to herself. This led to a lower self-esteem because integrity was such an important value to her.

The aftermath: Resurrecting your resentment

Eventually, it may be possible for the scapegoat survivor to know how oppressed they feel. When no longer dependent on the narcissistic parent, they can take stock of their own quality of life. The survivor sees how their inner life feels like a series of commands they must obey "or else".

These inner commands reflect what the survivor had to do to avoid the narcissistic parent's attacks. The survivor may have an inner narrative telling them they are going to be late for work. As they wake up in the morning, they grow increasingly anxious. Their inner voice is yelling more and more at them to "hurry up!".

The survivor may grow to feel like they are cooperating with their oppressor when they do tasks related to their own self-care. Getting to work on time can feel like a feeble act of obedience rather than acting out their own value of timeliness. Cleaning their home can feel like something they must do or feel like a terrible sloven person. Their narcissistic parent weaponized these tasks against them. Now, it can feel like the only reason to engage in these activities is to spare themselves the inner attack they will face if they do not do them. There is no real satisfaction to be felt - yet.

At this stage, the scapegoat survivor may recover a sacred form of protest. Instead of being left free to choose how they act, they had to do their parent's bidding. The survivor can now acknowledge that their worth is based on more than obedience.

Initially the survivor may direct their protest at themselves. It is they who are telling themselves to do this or that. They who are betraying their humanity by telling themselves to hurry up all the time. The only way to resist can often be to defy these inner commands. The survivor may show up late to work or not respond to phone calls or texts. These efforts are intended to restore their sense of freedom.

In her mid-twenties she had obtained enough distance from her narcissistic father to reflect on how she felt in her life. Until then, her inner world had to be a means to the end of limiting the dangers posed by her father. She started going to therapy because she knew her life was not working. We forged a good working relationship and she began talking about what her inner life felt like.

"When I get up in the morning I feel like I have an endless amount of things I have to do. Clean my apartment. Start work early. Make breakfast. I know this is all normal but it feels like someone is holding me

by the neck to do these things. Like if I don't, I'll be a disgrace to myself."

I asked, "Does this seem familiar to you?"

She said, "Yeah. I made my whole life about goals back since I was twelve. It made life seem possible. Just get the next good grade, do the next workout, or the next chore. Seemed like that gave me a fighting chance."

"Against what or who?" I asked.

"Seemed like me and the world," she answered.

"It also sounds similar to how insistent your father would be on doing his bidding. You had to treat yourself in the demanding way he treated you to protect yourself."

As treatment proceeded, Alexis felt a sense of acceptance from me. She felt like she had someone who understood her on her terms for the first time. This helped Alexis feel safe in looking at and questioning the commands she had formerly used to get by. For about a year in a five-year long treatment, Alexis expressed her protest. She worked out when she wanted to. She allowed herself to be a few minutes late to her sessions and to work. She allowed herself time where she had nothing to do. All of this was her protest against the inner tyranny of the commands of self-care.

Recovery: Relocating the betrayal from within to without

The process of recovery for someone who has endured this form of narcissistic abuse takes time. The survivor had to grant ownership of their abilities to take care of themselves to their narcissistic parent. It can take time, new relationships, and therapy to recover one's felt ownership of these abilities. The goal is to know that when they are, say, working to be punctual it is because they value this quality. They no longer have to do this solely to avoid a harsh rebuke from themselves or others.

Consider the tragic scenario where human traffickers abduct someone. These captors regard the trapped person as their property and feel entitled to exploit them. If their captive does not comply, then they face unbearable punishments. To survive, the captive must leverage their sexuality to meet the demands of their captives. The captive no longer gets to feel like they own this part of themselves.

If this captive escapes then their relationship to their own sexuality will take time to restore. They may feel like they betrayed themselves by using their sexuality in the ways they did to survive. Initially, they may avoid sexual contact with anyone. They may be too used to the inner scenario where sex means being domineered and enslaved.

I bring up this example because, in both cases, something inherently good had to be handed over to someone else. For the survivor of this kind of narcissistic abuse, it was their right to take care of themselves. For the human trafficking survivor, it was their sexuality. If and when this initial traumatic situation ends, both can initially feel betrayed by themselves. They see their efforts to be on time or to engage in sexual intimacy as selling themselves out.

With time and the experience of being treated as a deserving person, the survivor redefines how they were betrayed. The problem was not what they had to leverage to accommodate their domineering narcissistic parent. The betrayal occurred in the parent's dismissal of the *child's right* to be treated with respect and love. As this new definition of betrayal takes hold, survivors can feel deeper compassion and respect towards themselves. The part of them that figured out how to survive their narcissistic parent's betrayal of them is no longer at fault.

> *In the latter two years of treatment, Alexis was more used to the warmth, understanding and empathy she consistently found in treatment. She began to like herself. She saw herself to be as deserving as anyone else.*
>
> *"I've been thinking about what I want for myself," she said.*
>
> *"Oh yeah? Tell me."*
>
> *"I want to be around people who treat me the way I feel in here. I want to respect my feelings and those of people*

I care about. And certain goals at work are meaningful to me. I want to reach them.

"It sounds like that is coming from a place in you that gets to choose?"

"Yeah. I feel a lot less oppressed these days. I get why I had to treat myself that way. It was the only way to get through an impossible situation. But the problem was how I was treated, NOT how I coped."

18

When Learning About Narcissism Stops Being Helpful

> *Do you have an appetite for information about pathological narcissism that is never satisfied?*
> *Have you found diminishing returns in the helpfulness of this information?*
> *Do you find it hard to focus on yourself after a deep-dive on narcissism?*

People who realize they suffered narcissistic abuse can feel like Jim Carrey realizing his life is on TV in the movie the Truman Show. They can feel a sense of freedom and power in seeing that things were not what they seemed. They were not defective and undeserving as the narcissistic parent claimed. They felt this way because the narcissistic parent needed them to.

They may learn everything they can about narcissism. Anything to further clear up the fog they have had to live in. They are getting to make sense of what happened while in the throes of narcissistic abuse. At the same time, their quality of life may remain largely the same.

Past a certain point, immersing oneself in this information poses two risks. First, since the process of learning about narcissism is typically done alone, it can reinforce the assumption that you are all on your own. Second, it can strengthen the assumption that the narcissistic parent's opinion of you is more important than your own.

At long last: The first dose of information about narcissism

I cannot overstate the relief and clarity a survivor can feel when they realize their parent was narcissistic. They have had to live under the false premise that they were inferior and their parent was superior. Nobody likes to feel less-than. Understanding pathological narcissism shines a light on the path toward equal status.

The survivor gets to reframe their past. Whereas before, they may have recoiled in shame at how they were so disobedient, rude, or inconsiderate of their parent. Now they see that these accusations were the product of their parent's artificially inflated self-worth and entitled expectation that everyone reflect that elevated importance back to them. This can result in a loosening of a long-felt knot inside. The knot of forcing oneself to believe a lie that their survival depended on. In this case, the lie was that they were objectionable and their parent was perfect.

> Terence grew up feeling disconnected from his father. The man always seemed to have it all together but would not let Terence in. Nothing Terence did in his

own life interested his father. The only time Terence knew he existed to his father was when Terence approached him. Terence had no memory of his father seeking him out to spend time together.

At the same time, Terence felt a strong pull to show gratitude and appreciation for his father. If he did not make eye contact with his father whenever they were near, then his father would grow nonverbally irate. He would start slamming cabinet doors and criticize Terence for not picking up after himself. Terence knew he had to make a big show of appreciation towards his father or face this backlash.

His father mostly avoided social occasions and friendships. He would make up excuses for why he could not attend social functions. When forced to attend, he would occupy himself on his phone, making it impossible for other adults to talk to him.

Terence felt unaccompanied by his father throughout his childhood.

Occasionally, his father seemed taken by someone else and would go out of his way to make a good impression. He would shower them with attention and admiration. Terence would look on with the painful conclusion that he did not matter enough for his father to treat him so well.

The consequence for Terence was low self-worth and disappointment in what relationships offered. One day *he was perusing YouTube videos and stumbled upon one about covert narcissism. The speaker highlighted how such individuals tend to be aloof and avoidant yet entitled to others' warmth and admiration. This fit his experience with his father like a glove.*

Terence was overtaken with a sense of clarity and relief. He began to notice his own feelings of inner emptiness and longing. He could understand these feelings as a consequence of his father's dismissiveness. And he could understand his father's dismissiveness as a consequence of his father's psychological problems. This beat chalking it up to his own unworthiness.

How learning about narcissism may go too far

This phase of recovery can also happen in isolation from other people. The survivor can find books, articles, and videos that help them feel understood in what they have endured. After a lifetime of being deliberately misunderstood, this is invaluable.

Survivors' core trust in others may be shattered at this stage. They have learned that closeness means being deprived, devalued, and controlled. They have then had to believe they deserved such mistreatment to keep their most important relationship going. It is enough to make one want to be on one's own.

They have also had to organize their minds around the demands and needs of their narcissistic parent. Sure, this has not been a comfortable arrangement. But it has been an arrangement that beats no arrangement. In learning about narcissism, the survivor can keep the narcissistic parent in the center of their minds while finding their parent's claims about them to be faulty. This is a hopeful and marked improvement from the parent being in the center and being right about how unimportant the survivor is.

Learning about narcissistic abuse is a necessary but not sufficient step towards healing from it. It is one of three pillars of recovery. The other two pillars involve finding safe closeness to others and centering yourself in your mind. These cannot be accomplished without new experience.

Learning about pathological narcissism can go too far when it eclipses other aspects of the healing process. When this happens, it can unintentionally reinforce the survivor's assumptions that they are on their own and that it is their narcissistic parent who matters most in life.

> *With this liberating knowledge under his cap, Terence, immersed himself in more and more research on the topic. He read every book, blog and article he could find on covert narcissism. He watched videos of the sort too. Weeks stretched into months which stretched into a year and Terence was awash in understanding what was really happening in relationship to his father.*

> *At the same time, Terence still did not feel close to anyone in his life or like he could live based on his needs and goals. He had not entered therapy nor found a peer support group to help him. The prospect of doing either*

brought up dread and anxiety. 'What if they think I'm complaining over nothing?', 'What if they think I'm the real problem?', 'I just get too anxious and uncomfortable around others...'

Whenever Terence came up against these reservations, he would move back to the books and videos about narcissism. Perhaps there was more to learn that would make reaching out feel easier. He would feel relief from the dread and anxiety from earlier. As time wore on, however, he still did not reach out and found himself feeling alone and oriented around his father's psychology instead of his own.

The other two ingredients to healing

Finding and connecting with safe others

The survivor of a narcissistic parent has learned that they are on their own. A narcissistic parent is limited in empathy so their child rarely feels emotionally considered. At the same time the parent feels entitled for the child to show them attention and admiration. So the child must abandon what they need from the parent and tend to the parent's needs. Otherwise they face the narcissistic parent's vindictive wrath for failing to reflect back their importance. The child's existence on their own terms is unacknowledged. They are left to figure out life outside of their narcissistic parent completely on their own.

Here is why finding attuned and responsive friends and relationship partners is so important. In order to be our full selves we need to know that we will not lose the care of others. Otherwise we have to be too occupied with securing that care to turn to ourselves.

The path to finding and connecting to safe people is not easy for the survivor. It requires doing what used to lead to the trauma of abandonment and rejection. This includes reaching out to others, telling them what you need and do not need, and allowing yourself to expect good treatment from them.

Defying the narcissist's rules by turning your attention to yourself

A child is born expecting their parent to deliver all of the psychological and emotional necessities to become who they are. The child of a narcissistic parent gets little to none of these essentials. To survive, the child has to deny this fact and find a way to maintain hope that the parent can become who the child needs them to be. This often means doing what seems to please the parent. The child's hope is that if they can make the parent happy, then they will get the affirmation and love they want.

What makes the narcissistic parent happy is for the child to pay more attention to them than themselves. Unfortunately this is a one-way arrangement. No matter how much the child prioritizes the parent the job is never done. The parent keeps expecting more. So the child is left holding the bag.

It is important in the process of healing to eventually turn towards and prioritize one's own experience. There are plenty of aspects of a survivor's experience that are not about the narcissistic parent. These aspects deserve just as much attention as the parts that adapted to the parent.

The path to paying attention to oneself is also not easy for the survivor. It, too, requires doing what used to lead to the narcissistic parent's narcissistic rage and abandonment. The survivor can feel vulnerable to these same outcomes when doing this.

Terence eventually decided that he needed to try something new. He came to see me because I specialized in treating survivors of narcissistic abuse. Terence expected to go over his upbringing with a fine tooth comb with me. He was surprised to learn that most of my attention was on the person he was today. We talked about what he wanted out of his life and what stood in the way.

Terence worried that there was a right and wrong way to be a client and wondered if he was doing it "right". But I seemed equally interested in whatever he had to say. There did not seem to be a "wrong" way to be with me.

Terence brought up his lack of connection to safe others. We identified his fear of rejection as something that interfered with reaching out to them. Terence used his experience of my interest and appreciation in him to counter these fears. He identified a couple of friends in his life that seemed to treat him well yet whom he did not often make plans with. He deliberately began reaching out to them and cultivated an ongoing friendship with them. They showed interest in him and his life and offered him support for whatever was important to him.

After a while, Terence realized that he had not looked at a book or video on narcissism in quite some time. He reflected on how useful this information was for him. He was also grateful to be focused on new safe people and himself.

I encourage you to exercise compassion and patience with yourself if you find this applies to you. I do not want to be judgmental if indexing on learning about narcissism is still an important piece to your process of recovery. Ultimately shifting from this pillar of recovery to the others can be liberating. It also needs to feel survivable. If that time has not yet arrived, then I strongly encourage compassion and patience with yourself. That stance towards yourself does wonders and may even make it feel safer sooner than later to incorporate the other two pillars.

Pillar #2:

Gaining Distance from Narcissistic Abusers (and Closeness to Safe People)

19

Choosing And Protecting Safe Relationships with The Second Pillar of Recovery

> *Do you find yourself in friendships or relationships where kindness is hard to come by?*
> *Do you avoid people who are good to you because you think they must not really know you or there must be something 'wrong' with them?*
> *Do you expect to be rejected if your opinion does not match the other person's?*

Scapegoat survivors of narcissistic parents may actually feel better when they are in one-sided relationships. The reason goes back to how uncared for they were as a child leading them to feel abandoned, anguished, and astray. I will call these the "Three A's" as we go along. To avoid the Three A's the scapegoat child had to find a way to stay hopeful their parent could and would care for them if they could earn it. By adopting unconscious beliefs that they are defective and undeserving, the child protects this hope. Now when they experience the Three A's it is just because they are not earning their parent's love the way they should be. Their parent remains capable in the child's mind of providing what is needed. Although the child rarely receives actual care they can feel hopeful they will get it when they are around the parent.

As discussed in Chapter Four, the scapegoat child internalizes this pattern of interaction with their narcissistic parent. In so doing, they feel buffered from the Three A's when they are psychologically close to that parent and exposed to these feelings when they are not. Staying close can mean acting like that parent is around and in charge or treating oneself the same way the parent mistreated them. Scapegoat survivors do one or both by moving toward people today who treat them like they do not deserve much. Such friendships and relationships reinforce their internal connection to their narcissistic parent. And this internal connection staves off the ongoing threat of the Three A's.

Reciprocal friendships and relationships can feel threatening to the scapegoat survivor at first. This is because being treated well makes them feel distant from their internalized narcissistic parent. If they feel distant then they are at risk of feeling the Three A's. These safe friends and partners may offer care not available earlier in life. However the past trauma of not having it available can initially flood the survivor with the Three A's. This makes it very difficult - at first - to see that things can be different now.

The second Pillar of Recovery from narcissistic abuse involves moving away from narcissistically abusive people and towards safe people. The *challenge* of doing this is re-encountering the feelings of being ashamed, abandoned, and astray that arise when moving away from your internalized narcissistic parent. The *promise* of doing this is a gradual realization that the care you need from others will no longer be withdrawn at any moment.

How staying close to the internalized narcissistic parent protects the scapegoat child

A narcissistic parent does not show the scapegoat child love but instead uses them to maintain their own flagging self-esteem. If the child cooperates then they get to feel useful to the parent and therefore hopeful the parent will eventually provide the care the child needs. If the child does not cooperate and, say, expects actual care from the narcissistic parent then they feel something far worse. The child faces the actual absence of care the narcissistic parent has to offer without the anesthesia of hope for something different. Such encounters can throw the child into one or more of the Three A's.

Abandoned

The scapegoat child's healthy need to know that they are genuinely important to their parent does not get met. Instead they find a parent who is not interested nor genuinely concerned about them. The scapegoat child may get some attention for superficial attributes. However, they feel utterly alone in their inner worlds. They feel abandoned.

Roy always felt a pressure inside to be doing or thinking something. If he paused, he would feel a terrible state come over him. From the moment he awoke to when he went to sleep he felt like he had to stay ahead of this feeling. Action in thought or deed was the only thing that had worked for him.

Eventually Roy grew to understand that the feeling he had been running from was that of abandonment. In therapy, we traced this to how unseen and uncared for he felt in his home growing up. His father was narcissistic and treated Roy as if he could not do anything right. His mother was emotionally uninvolved and paid him little attention. As Roy grew closer to me and certain caring friends in his life he was able to see how abandoned he felt in relation to his parents.

Anguished

The scapegoat child who does not find a way to stay close to their narcissistic parent faces anguish. This is a state of self-loathing guilt brought on by a lapse in the child's loyalty to the narcissistic parent. The child typically feels responsible for the parent's emotional well-being when it should be the other way around. They are burdened with the conclusion that what they do or do not do will make or break the parent. If the child acts in ways that supposedly break the parent then they will feel a torrent of self-blame and guilt for supposedly hurting their parent[3]. The scapegoat child who stays close to their actual and internalized narcissistic parent is spared such guilt.

> *Roy knew to never ask for anything. Nonetheless he worried that he required too much from others. He was a good employee at his company but during performance reviews he expected to be told that he needed too much help to get his work done. Although his supervisors never told him this he kept expecting it.*
>
> *When his partner would host parties Roy did not feel safe to pause and converse with guests that he liked. He felt compelled to constantly check whether everyone had enough food or drink. If nobody needed anything he would identify and solve potential problems.*
>
> *In therapy we understood how being useful to his guests helped stave off the anguish he would feel if he did what he wanted at these parties.*

Astray

The scapegoat child who does not make themselves useful to the narcissistic parent can feel profoundly disoriented and astray. As painful as being close to the narcissistic parent is, it is also orienting. The scapegoat child knows what to anticipate and how to react when engaged with this parent.

---

[3] This sequence of steps involving a child feeling responsibility for a parent are brilliantly laid out in Engel & Ferguson's book: "Imaginary Crimes". You can find the citation in the References section of this book.

Since the narcissistic parent does not benignly stay in contact with the scapegoat child when they go their own direction, the child can feel painfully astray. The child is psychologically lost in these moments without hope of being found.

> *Roy found it difficult to speak up in groups of people. He would let others set the conversational agenda even if he had something he wanted to discuss. He also had friends who seemed eager talk more than listen to him.*
>
> *One day at work, Roy was in a meeting with three people who had always seemed to appreciate him. One colleague asked Roy to share his thoughts about the project they were discussing because they were sure that Roy had some good ideas. As inviting as this seemed, Roy suddenly felt tongue tied. His mind went blank and he did not know what to say. He felt astray.*

Staying psychologically close to their narcissistic parent protects the scapegoat child and survivor from the Three A's. This means not expecting care from others and being useful to them. Doing this produces a less intense but ongoing dull pain that can be lived with.

The challenge of the second pillar

The second Pillar of Recovery involves moving away from narcissistically abusive people and towards safe people. This allows the scapegoat survivor to reawaken their need to be cared for. As important as this is to heal, it is also challenging. Forsaking this need keeps the scapegoat survivor psychologically close to their narcissistic parent and away from the Three A's. Embracing it can require the survivor to re-encounter the Three A's. This time, however, there can be a different ending to these difficult states.

The promise of the second pillar

The scapegoat child had to avoid the Three A's because there would be no end to the pain involved. They were stuck with their narcissistic parent and could not get the care that would have truly mended these states. When the scapegoat survivor puts the second Pillar of Recovery into practice there is a new hope. Now the safe other people they move towards can - in fact - offer the care they have been seeking.

This does not mean that the scapegoat survivor will not have to re-encounter the Three A's. It does mean that re-encountering these painful states can eventually yield to a quality of life that feels much safer and fulfilling. Here is how:

1. The scapegoat survivor begins to notice who treats them well and who does not in their life.
2. They spend more time and energy with the latter and less with the former.
3. They move away from being useful to others and towards expecting care from them.

4. They can feel abandoned, anguished and astray as they do this.
5. While they encounter the Three A's they remain in connection to these new safe friends and partners.
6. These new ongoing connections gradually inform the survivor that they can expect and get care as needed today.
7. As the scapegoat survivor grows convinced of this new information they can tolerate the Three A's more easily while enjoying a different and more real form of connection to others.

In short, the problem becomes the solution. Initially, safe others need to be avoided because that meant moving away from one's internalized narcissistic parent and experiencing the Three A's. As the survivor moves towards them today, however, they gradually experience the benefits of being treated well. Over time, the hope for the internalized parent to give what you have yet to receive from them can give way to the ongoing actual experience of care and respect from the safe people around you.

What to expect in this section

You will find validating and compassionate explanations for why it can feel so difficult to move away from a narcissistic parent, partner, or friend. You will learn how to assert boundaries to protect yourself from narcissistically abusive people today. And, you will understand how to take advantage of the freedom and healthy entitlement that relationships with safe people can offer you.

20

A Tell-Tale Sign of Safe People for Scapegoat Survivors of Narcissistic Parents

> *Do you worry that others will feel abandoned if you are not constantly paying attention to them?*
> *Does it seem like others are emotionally empty and depend on you to stay afloat?*
> *Do you feel overwhelming guilt when you pursue your own happiness?*

These questions reflect a fact of life for scapegoat children of narcissistic parents. Kids in this position realize that Mom or Dad do not have much inside of them. They depend on the people around them to fill them up. Their narcissistic parent's life is lived from the outside in.

Their parent's inner emptiness stresses the child in two ways. First, all children want to know that their parent is OK on their own. The child of a narcissistic parent knows this is not true and wants to protect the parent – often unconsciously. They have to assume responsibility for their parent's psychological well-being. Life under this assumption is inherently stressful because they have little control over their parent's well-being.

Second, the child cannot pursue their own development because they fear - and are told that - this harms the narcissistic parent. The parent is empty and needs their child to show them admiration and obedience at all times to feel full. This means that the child's own desires, goals, and relationships have to take a backseat.

The child is left alone with themselves. They only feel like they have a viable parent when they are filling that parent's cup. The good news is that not everyone is empty like this.

Safe people can take care of themselves even when others are not tending to them. This does not mean that safe people are super happy inside. It just means that they have the psychological strength to own their problems. They do not feel entitled that others solve them. In contrast, narcissistically abusive people feel empty and coerce others to keep them full.

Having to fill your narcissistic parent's emptiness

The child is born into the job of filling their narcissistic parent's inner emptiness. This job description can get communicated in subtle ways. The young child may feel like all is well when they are looking at their parent. Both may be smiling and seem happy. The child may sense something disturbing and different when they look away. The child can make the parent happy by turning back towards them and smiling. Although it is a seemingly 'easy fix' it comes at great cost to the child.

The child has to force themselves to act in ways they do not want to. They have to look at the parent even though they want to look away to have a moment to themselves. This makes the child feel like they are not in possession of themselves. Now the child has to look to the parent to know what they should do rather than themselves.

How life feels when others' happiness takes priority

Amanda felt inner pressure to keep others happy at all times. She tried to do this through humor, caretaking or acts of service. Although these are good qualities, they tyrannized her. She could never rest from these duties. To do so would invite a flood of anxiety that she had not done something she should have.

Her romantic relationships tended to follow a common trajectory. She found herself attracted to men who seemed unhappy in their own lives. She felt exhilarated when she could brighten their demeanor even for a moment. These moments of exhilaration would lead her into relationships with some of these men.

Her life in these relationships would get smaller and smaller as her partner demanded more and more of her. She was implicitly forbidden from asking anything of them. She would constantly worried about them. Her partner's happiness was all that was allowed to matter in the relationship. And they could be made unhappy by the slightest lapse in her attention to them. For example, she found herself apologizing for taking ten minutes to return a text.

Amanda grew up with a narcissistic father who provided the blueprint for putting others before herself. He was a prominent psychologist who loved to tell her about his successes at work. She knew that when he turned to her to say these things she had to show rapt attention. Any sign that she was less than amazed at his accomplishments and he would seethe with contempt. He would never tell her directly that she did not meet his exorbitant needs. He would just stop talking to her and walk out of the room. Then he would barely speak to her for the rest of the day. These times felt awful for Amanda and she resolved to do whatever she had to do to prevent them.

Children of narcissistic parents like Amanda must abandon important developmental goals of their own. They have to assume responsibility for the parent's emotional well-being. The next step from assuming responsibility is concluding that what the child does or does not do can make or break the parent (Engel & Ferguson, 2004). Then if the child does or does not do what supposedly breaks the parent they feel at fault. A torrent of self-blame and guilt can then flood the child.

To prevent such outcomes children of narcissistic parents can unconsciously adopt beliefs like:
- Others' needs are more important than my own.

- To be close to others I have to make them the center of my world.
- I must care for others or they will fall apart.
- I must care for others or they will punish me.

Amanda adopted the belief that to be close to others she had to make them the center of her world. This made relationships depleting and strenuous for her. Such beliefs are called 'pathogenic'. They solve the immediate problem of keeping their narcissistic parent happy. Outside the home they create psychological suffering because they constrict the person from being their full selves. Amanda in this case could not pursue her own happiness.

Grant yourself permission to center your happiness

After surviving this type of childhood it is essential to consider that most people are not empty like a narcissistic parent. At first, this may just seem like an idea that *feels* completely untrue. This is because the very world you lived in with your parent depended on you filling them up. We cannot quickly switch out one world for another. It takes time and corrective experience to do so.

The second Pillar of Recovery from narcissistic abuse is to find and move towards safe relationships. An important marker of what makes someone safe is their ability to care for themselves. This means that when you care for yourself they do not take this as a slight. They expect you to care for yourself just as they do for themselves.

When a friend, partner or therapist embodies this ability to care for their own needs then you get to challenge the beliefs discussed above. This is because it is now safe to do so. You get to know that these relationships do not depend on you taking responsibility for someone else's happiness.

5 signs of a safe relationship

1. The other does not grow hostile if you decline an invitation.
2. The other does not take great offense to the occasional interruption when speaking.
3. The other is concerned but not offended if you express frustration or hurt with a way they treated you.
4. In group settings, this person does not insist that you only pay attention to them.
5. The other person shows genuine interest in what is important to you.

This list is not exhaustive but can serve as a starting point for identifying relationships today that feel safe.

> *Amanda did have one friend, named Claire who always felt different to her. Claire was generally happy to see Amanda but did not seem to expect much from her. That is, Amanda rarely felt like she owed something to*

Claire if they did not talk for a couple weeks. Claire just did not operate in this way.

Claire was studying to get her post-bac in business administration and had a steady relationship wither her boyfriend. She always seemed self-directed but open to connection with Amanda. She showed interest in Amanda's life beyond her troubled relationships. They would meet for dinner and discuss topics of mutual interest. Amanda left these dinners feeling more comfortable in her own skin than usual.

As she reflected on the difference between how she felt with Claire versus her boyfriend she realized that Claire did not expect Amanda to fill her up. She seemed to do that for herself and this helped Amanda feel free to do the same. Amanda wondered, "If some people are like Claire then maybe it is unfair for my boyfriend to expect so much and give so little."

Now when her boyfriend grew demanding because Amanda was not attending to him she felt more anger than guilt. She had experience with Claire that defied her belief about being close. With Claire she could feel close without making her the center of her world. She knew this felt way better than how she felt with her boyfriend. Her tolerance for his demands decreased. Eventually she decided to break up with him to find a relationship that felt more like her friendship with Claire.

21

The Science Behind Gaining Distance from The Narcissistic Abuser

> *Do you feel physiologically different when you are around a narcissistic abuser?*
> *Do you wonder if you are making these feelings up?*
> *Do you feel guilt when you move away from people who make you feel ill at ease?*

There is a scientific explanation for why the second Pillar of Recovery is so important. Our minds and nervous systems adjust to how we are treated in close relationships. When we can be around people who feel safe, our nervous system seeks to engage with them. When we are around people who feel dangerous then our nervous system works to protect us. If the dangerous person expects us to appear socially engaged then we may be forced to close down on the inside and seem engaged on the outside. But there is no fooling our nervous systems. When the system signals that we are around someone dangerous we cannot argue ourselves out of it.

A narcissistically abusive parent can activate the protective function of your nervous system. Being in such a physiologically closed state is hard. Everything can feel like it takes effort, you feel all alone, there is a constant sense that something bad is about to happen, and it is nearly impossible to relax. Creating distance from an abusive person is an act of self-care. In this chapter, I explain the science that supports this claim.

Evolution prepared us to seek safe people and avoid dangerous ones

We have a vast network of connected cells that send electrical signals intended to adapt to our immediate circumstances. Taken together, these networks are called the nervous system. There are lots of sub-nervous systems that address specific functions.

One of these sub-nervous-systems that inform what we automatically do, feel, and sense is called the Autonomic Nervous System (ANS). The cells in the ANS go all over our body. They play a big role in dictating what our internal state feels like.

The ANS has 3 sub-systems from oldest to newest – evolutionarily speaking.

1. The oldest subsystem causes us to freeze in response to threats where fight or flight will not work.
2. The second newest subsystem activates our fight-or-flight responses when appropriate.
3. The newest allows social engagement and controls our gaze, tone of speech, and ability to listen.

When activated each sub-system produces a different corresponding internal state. The social engagement subsystem produces a state of connection, well-being, and presence. The fight-

or-flight subsystem produces a state of alarm, readiness, and hypervigilance. The freeze subsystem produces a state of dissociation, lifelessness, and absence.

There is a hierarchy to these three subsystems. In order for the social communication subsystem to activate, the other two subsystems must be de-activated. Similarly, in order for the fight-or-flight system to activate the freeze system must be de-activated.

How do our nervous systems determine if we are safe or not?

Everything I am describing today comes from the Polyvagal Theory. This theory was developed by Stephen Porges. He makes the case that our nervous systems communicate with one another to signal whether the other person is safe or not (2009). Via the other's facial cues, vocal tone, and eye contact the three subsystems determine which is most appropriate for the situation. Porges calls this process neuroception and it happens outside of our awareness.

Sensing – or neurocepting - safety is an involuntary experience. These three subsystems tell us whether we are safe – we do not tell our nervous systems that we are safe. It is why Bessel Van Der Kolk might say the body keeps the score. There is no fooling our nervous systems about who is safe and who is not.

Applying the polyvagal theory to recovery from narcissistic abuse

f you were born to a narcissistic parent then your nervous system had to cope with danger from an early age. The dangers of being devalued, deprived and controlled by the narcissistic parent were ever present. So, your fight-or-flight and freeze nervous subsystems had to work overtime in relationship to this parent.

Appraisal of the dangers by your nervous system is involuntary. Survivors of such abuse may find that it is the mere physical or mental presence of the parent that can set off these internal alarms. And the survivor can be powerless to convince their nervous system otherwise. To prevent these two defensive subsystems from getting activated we must limit exposure to the sources of danger. We cannot be in the presence of the narcissistic abuser and tell our nervous subsystems not to be alarmed. This is the first component of gaining distance – removing immediate sources of danger from your life.

There is a second component to gaining distance. If your nervous system was primed to perceive danger then you may be biased towards it in ambiguous situations. So when someone who is otherwise safe does something on the borderline between safety and danger, the survivor can err on the side of danger. This can be the legacy of trauma. In order to prevent unsurvivable outcomes, we had to presume danger to anticipate and limit the damage of these events. It was adaptive to do so.

With enough distance from your narcissistic parent, you can recalibrate your safety vs danger appraisal system. This recalibration takes place with people who are otherwise safe people to be close to. It is an ongoing process that takes time but is well worth it.

Therapy is a great place to start. A therapist offers you interpersonal signals that help your nervous system determine you are safe. A therapist's job is to remain in their social engagement nervous subsystem. This offers the client a reliable and consistent source of safety. If the client has a history of narcissistic abuse then their two defensive subsystems may still kick in at times. In therapy the client and therapist can ride those episodes out together. The goal is for the client to return to feeling safe again with the therapist.

> *Joanne was in therapy to recover from growing up with a physically abusive narcissistic father. She went unprotected from this abuse throughout her childhood. We had established a good working relationship. Joanne felt safe most of the time in her sessions.*
>
> *About three months into treatment, she started the session off by discussing a realization she had about a sibling. She realized that this person held a disparaging attitude toward her. Joanne said she was going to protect herself from such treatment by limiting contact. After saying this, she suddenly experienced me to be scrutinizing her with my gaze. She wanted to hide from*

me. She had trouble thinking clearly. She felt outside of herself yet stuck in my cross-hairs.

I said, "It's as if you feel taken over right now. I wonder if this is at all what it was like when your father would look at you silently?" I linked her intent to protect herself from this sibling with feeling endangered. She was gaining distance from someone who was dangerous - something she was not allowed to do earlier in her life. Such changes can feel dangerous for the nervous system at first.

Joanne felt some relenting within herself. She said, "Yeah, maybe. This state is all around me right now. It feels so complete." As more time elapsed, she felt a shift. She could now reflect on what happened with me. "Wow, that came out of the blue. Suddenly, you were a scary scrutinizer, not the person I've known these past three months."

In this example, Joanne started the session in her social engagement subsystem. She grew alarmed after expressing her intent to protect herself from her sibling's derision. This alarm seemed to push her into the freeze nervous subsystem. She felt stuck and unable to escape my scrutiny. I maintained my socially engaged presence towards her. This allowed her nervous system to pick up on this, so she could shift back up to her socially engaged mode. Once there, we could begin to make sense of what had happened.

As these types of sequences happen over and over, clients get to know that their time spent in the defensive subsystems does not have to be permanent anymore. Now, there is the opportunity to continue taking in information and returning to a state of social engagement with people who are safe.

22

Restoring Your Boundaries After Narcissistic Intrusions

> *Did you have to 'drop everything' when your parent walked into a room and pay attention to them?*
> *Do you show appreciation when someone shares their opinion about your choices - even if you disagree?*
> *When someone takes over something you are doing does it feel impossible to tell them to stop?*

One of the ways that narcissists negatively impact others is through their intrusiveness. They regard their own ideas, opinions and perceptions as superior and others' as inferior. So, they confuse intruding on said others with their point of view with doing them a 'favor'. In the narcissist's mind they are gifting the inferior person with "guidance" that will make the other's life better. The other person must show gratitude or face the narcissist's wrath or withdrawal.

This feature of narcissistic psychology is particularly harmful for the scapegoat child. The narcissistic parent uses this child to embody the intolerable worthlessness within themselves. This process of devaluing the scapegoat child often includes regular intrusions. The scapegoat child has no choice but to permit these intrusions. The child's survival strategy comes at the expense of getting to feel like they are in charge of themselves.

To adapt to the narcissistic parent's intrusions the child must adopt the unconscious belief that others' needs are more important than their own. The narcissistic parent's needs include finding the scapegoat child to be inadequate. So it is not just others' needs for care that are more important but others' needs to devalue the child.

The narcissistic parent's 'right' to intrude

Ed was a 25-year-oldear old bicycle mechanic who was in therapy because he did not feel like the author of his own life. He described his father as someone who was obsessed with status. If his father perceived a work colleague to show him anything but deference he would feel wounded. His father would come home and take up the family's dinnertime with stories of how terrible this colleague was. When Ed was in seventh grade, his father would take to scrutinize Ed about his school performance. Was he doing his homework? What were his latest test grades? And so on. If Ed answered that he got anything less than 100% on a test his father would say, "OK, I want to see how you're doing your homework after dinner". These sessions may have seemed helpful on the surface but Ed's experience told him otherwise. His father would drone on and tell Ed how he was not doing this and that properly. His father was going to do

> him the 'favor' of showing him how to get his grades back 'on track'. His father would then ask questions he knew Ed did not know and act astonished that Ed could be so "dumb". These sessions went on for two hours until his father felt sufficiently superior. They were excruciating for Ed.
>
> In therapy, we broke down more of what Ed's experience was in these moments. He knew that if he protested his father's 'help' that he would be in for a world of hurt. His father would grow enraged and say that Ed was an ungrateful kid who would never amount to anything. That was always scary and hurtful. So, Ed knew that his father needed to be agreed with when he intruded upon Ed with his opinions like this. When Ed went along, his father seemed content.

Ed's father illustrates how a narcissistic parent will intrude upon their child. His father did this to restore his own sense of superiority that got punctured at work. There are three reasons the narcissistic parent does this:

1) Intruding boosts the narcissistic parent's sense of superiority

By believing they have a right to intrude they reinforce their sense of superiority to the child. This is a very important outcome to achieve for the narcissistic parent. Their self-worth is inflated yet fragile. This was demonstrated in how easily wounded Ed's father could be. Reinflating their self-worth often happens by intruding into the scapegoat child's life. Doing so means that the parent's needs are more important than the child's needs.

2) The narcissistic parent sees the child as an extension of themselves

he narcissistic parent uses other people to manage their exhaustive self-esteem needs. They do not see other people as separate persons who deserve respect, interest and support. When a parent intrudes upon their child's life they are seeing that child the way they want to. They are not seeing the child based on what the child indicates they need in that moment. And the way the parent wants to perceive the child is as a broken-down person in dire need of the parent's "help".

3) The scapegoat child learns their boundaries are meaningless

The impact of these intrusions on the scapegoat child is that they learn it is futile to say 'No'. Doing so only results in indignant rage or hostile withdrawal by the parent. Harmony with the narcissistic parent requires the scapegoat child to surrender their boundaries. They do not have a right to object when someone else wants something from them. As the child operates this way, the narcissistic parent can more easily see themselves as superior and the child as an extension of themselves.

The scapegoat child's dilemma

Children have an inherent need to see a gleam in their parent's eye when they walk in the room. Such experiences let the child know that their existence is welcome and cherished. This is an essential ingredient to developing an authentic self that feels loveable. The child of a narcissistic parent does not experience this.

Although the child does not receive the narcissistic parent's gleam they still want to know they can make the parent happy. The narcissistic parent may react with goodwill - or at least the absence of ill-will - when the child permits these intrusions. Ed's father seemed pleased when Ed reacted appreciatively to his "guidance". This may be the best the scapegoat child can hope for. The narcissistic parent's happiness is a self-centered one. The parent is happy when others comply and unhappy when they do not. Allowing the parent's intrusions is the closest the child can come to making their parent happy with them.

The scapegoat child's dilemma is that the parent's intrusions are offensive but a boundary will only make the parent unhappy with them. Making the parent unhappy has two bad consequences for the child:

1. they face the parent's wrath or withdrawal, and
2. they may feel unlovable by not making the parent happy with them.

On the other hand if they do what makes the parent happy they make themselves unhappy. That is, they lose a sense of their right to choose when they say No or Yes. The child needs a solution to this dilemma.

The scapegoat child's solution

Children with an intrusive narcissistic parent can solve this dilemma by adopting the unconscious belief that others needs are more important than their own. Now the narcissistic parent is doing nothing wrong by ignoring the child's boundaries. What the parent needs takes precedence over what the child's needs.

When the scapegoat child adopts this belief they face a particularly insidious situation. The role of the scapegoat child is to embody the worthless feelings the narcissistic parent feels but cannot tolerate. So the parent's need in this case is for the child to feel less than the parent. The child has to facilitate the parent's cruelty towards them because the parent's needs are what is important.

If the child was not in the scapegoat role then the parent's needs would be less malevolent. Yes, it would be problematic for the child to have to put the parent's emotional wellbeing before their own. And the child could conclude within themselves that they are worth less than the parent. But when the parent's need is for the scapegoat child to feel worse than the parent then the child must sacrifice their wellbeing for the parent. Doing so meets the parent's cruel 'need.'

As this persists, the scapegoat child may come to associate intrusiveness with connection. The belief that others' needs are more important may lead them toward exploitative people. Having a friend or partner who intrudes on them is familiar. Putting up with such treatment may come with a sense of relief that they will not be attacked nor abandoned.

> *At Ed's job he found himself freezing up whenever the bike shop's owner came around. In therapy, he described feeling like it was inevitable that the owner would find a flaw in Ed's work and take over. Ed might even try to get ahead of this and ask the owner a question about how to do this or that.*

> *We discussed how Ed's presentation of himself as not knowing as much as the owner was useful. If the owner's intrusion felt inevitable, then doing this would minimize its disruptive effects. The cost was Ed's sense of competence at his job and the owner's perception of his competence. However, Ed had learned from his father that others want to see him as incompetent so they can intrude with demonstrations of how to be competent.*

Recovering your boundaries

The scapegoat child learned that their parent grew hostile or distant when they said "No". The best way to practice setting boundaries is to do so with people who react with warmth and connection. Doing so allows your system to de-couple boundaries from getting rejected. You learn that your boundaries can enhance good relationships.

With such practice under your belt it can be easier to set boundaries in toxic relationships. In these relationships it is likely that the other will be rejecting in response. If you suffered traumatic levels of rejection from a narcissistic parent then this can be re-traumatizing. It often does not matter how healthy you "know" it is to set boundaries with a toxic person.

New experiences of it being safe to set boundaries create a new belief. Scapegoat survivors see that boundaries help others meet their needs. Once this new belief is established the reaction of a toxic person to boundaries may feel less re-traumatizing. The survivor is not setting a boundary while thinking they are committing an offense. Now they set the boundary with the toxic person as though they are giving that person a gift that should enhance their relationship. If the toxic person rejects this gift, then that reflects on them, not the scapegoat survivor.

> *His father continued to intrude into Ed's life by baiting him into discussions about finances. He might ask Ed whether he was saving for retirement. Ed would enthusiastically reply that he was. No matter what Ed said, his father would then tell him that he should be doing it differently. Ed had to hold his own financial judgments in low regard to put up with his father's intrusive criticism.*

In therapy, Ed got to see how unreasonable and unwarranted his father's intrusiveness was. Ed's own feelings had always told him this but he had learned to view them as invalid. I worked to support Ed's feelings of offense towards his father's intrusions.

One day in therapy, Ed said, "I was so mad. On the phone with my Dad he brought up finances again and implied that I don't know what I'm doing. He laughed mockingly and asked if I had any other 'bright ideas' about what stocks to pick rather than invest in real estate like he does."
I said, "You were offended. Rightly so. Have you given any thought to how you might protect yourself from these kinds of insults from your father?"

Ed said, "Well, not really. I mean that's just how he is."

"You're right. Does that mean that you have to put up with being treated poorly though?"
Ed said, "I mean no. But I worry that I'll hurt his feelings if I do."

I said, "Yeah, I bet. That makes a lot of sense. I think to stay connected to your father you had to make his feelings your top priority. This helped you keep him happy with you as a kid and was necessary."

This led to us talking more about and questioning Ed's sense of responsibility for his father's emotions at the expense of his own. Over time Ed grew to see telling his father how he wanted to be treated as an act of protection that he deserved to take. On one of their phone calls this change was evident:

Ed's father asked him to share about his retirement savings and Ed said, "You know, Dad, I would rather not. Those matters are personal to me and I want to keep them that way."
His father said, "Oh come on. What is this? What has gotten into you? I asked a harmless question and here you go getting all uptight about it."

Ed felt a tinge of shame and doubt over whether he had made too big a deal out of this. But he stayed the course and said, "Look, this just something I've decided. If you want to keep talking about something else, great. If you continue to browbeat me into talking about my finances then I am going to hang up and we can talk another time."

Ed's heart was beating hard and his palms sweated as he said this. To his surprise, hi father's tone de-escalated and he said, "Alright, alright. So, did you see the game last night?"

Not every attempt to set boundaries will go as well as it did for Ed. The key is to know in a new safe relationship – such as therapy - that you are not responsible for others' emotional well-being. With this knowledge you can feel justified in asserting boundaries. If the other person protests you do not have to waver. Their upset is no longer your problem.

23

Closeness Without Confinement After Narcissistic Abuse

> *Does it feel impossible to live life without orienting to external demands?*
> *Do you find it difficult to know what you want for yourself?*
> *Do you wonder what the outcome of recovery from narcissistic abuse should look and feel like?*

The scapegoat child's most pressing issue is to feel like their parent is willing to be there for them. It is a fulltime job to convince themselves of this. This job requires a lot of denial and effort to be who that parent needs them to be. In exchange the child gets temporary relief from the gnawing reality that their narcissistic parent is incapable of doing this.

The scapegoat child learned that having someone there meant being emotional nourishment for the other. Relationships where two people are equally important offer something different. Now each person is responsible for nourishing themselves but nobody is alone. It is a process and sometimes a challenge to get used to this.

Scapegoat survivors can move from closeness feeling coercive to empowering. There are two components to this healing process. First is structuring one's environment to prevent further harm. Second is switching from the life purpose of avoiding catastrophic isolation to pursuing what you need and want. This means discovering an entirely new way of being close to others. A way that does not require sacrifice of yourself but offers mutual benefit. You get to take the other's *willingness* to be there for granted. This allows you to remain in contact with yourself while being with them. I will describe the process of making this switch and use an anonymized case example to illustrate.

2 components that lead to empowered closeness

The first component is to restructure your environment to prevent further harm. As the saying goes: "Safety First". This restructuring is necessary to undo prior learning. The scapegoat child learned that catastrophic aloneness occurs when they do not meet their narcissistic parent's coercive demands. The scapegoat child who - rightfully - expects their parent to meet their needs faces this kind of aloneness. So, the child learns that a really bad outcome happens if they expect to be treated well. They also learn they can prevent that bad outcome by expecting nothing and giving everything to their narcissistic parent.

The scapegoat survivor must restructure their environment to remove situations and people that reinforce the old learning. They must also populate their environment with people and experiences that allow for new learning.

This first component is what the three Pillars of Recovery are all about. The first pillar of making sense of what happened allows you to become more aware of the old learning. The second Pillar offers tactics to move away from those who reinforce the old learning and towards those who do not. And the third Pillar - living in defiance of the narcissist's rules - facilitates experiences of adequacy and deservedness without losing the goodwill of important others in their life.

Living for fulfillment means switching the goal of life from avoiding catastrophic aloneness to being fully yourself. To do so, the scapegoat survivor must be convinced their most important relationships will not be threatened. They can take others' goodwill towards them for granted and pursue what brings them fulfillment.

> *Jennifer grew up with a narcissistic mother who intruded into most aspects of her life. When Jennifer was at home, her mother would barge into her room and demand she finish her chores. These chores made up an exhaustive list that seemed impossible to Jennifer to ever get done.*
>
> *Jennifer's adolescence was marred by getting berated at home then having to serve out long sentences of being grounded. Her friendships and relationships at school suffered because she could not socialize outside of school. She found herself feeling like her time was not*

her own. She would make schedules for herself that detailed what she was going to do and accomplish in her 'free' time. Earmarking time to study and exercise gave her a semblance of feeling like her time was her own. She could only schedule activities that kept her at home or she would have been a target for her mother's attack.

Jennifer moved away to go to college. In her first year she took an abnormal psychology class and had to do a report on narcissistic personality disorder. As she was doing research she stumbled upon the reddit thread 'raisedbynarcissists'. She saw the first heading: "Did your Nparent yell at you about chores?" and went on to read about someone describing something that was almost exactly what she suffered. She found more and more points in common on this thread. She felt like a new portal in the world had opened. One where she might not be the problem. Her mind could only get glimpses of this portal. It upended too much of what she had taken as fact for so long.

This moment led her to find and consume as much information as she could about narcissistic abuse. She learned that a narcissistic person often acts intrusively in relationships. She saw in her mother the sense of entitlement that led to treating Jennifer like her property.

It all made so much sense. But Jennifer still struggled with feeling constricted and worth less than others. She knew that she needed help and sought therapy. She told me about her discovery from reddit. Jennifer got to tell her story to another human being for the first time in her life. It felt strange, anxiety-provoking, and somewhat relieving.

Jennifer would work with me for the rest of her time as an undergraduate. We developed a new frame of reference for what Jennifer could and should expect from others. Jennifer found her feelings of hurt and resentment at one particular friend's dismissiveness validated by me. Instead of seeing herself as too sensitive Jennifer located the issue in her friend's lack of emotional generosity. Jennifer began moving away from such people in her life. She also found herself moving towards people who seemed to like her and wanted to be around her. In Jennifer's senior year, she began to question her schedule-making practice. She grew curious how her days might go if she did not so rigorously control her time. When she noticed the impulse to create a schedule, she shifted her attention to something else. Over time, she felt freer.

Jennifer put the three Pillars of Recovery into action in her life. She made sense of what happened in a way that located the problem in her mother's psychopathology instead of her bad character. She moved away from her mother's narcissistic abuse and her dismissive friend. She moved towards friends who readily liked her. And she defied her mother's narcissistic rule that her time was not her own.

Overcoming what closeness used to mean

In order for the scapegoat child to feel like their narcissistic parent was there, they had to sacrifice themselves. This meant being who the parent required them to be. The scapegoat child learned that taking on their narcissistic parent's bad feelings maximized the parent's viability as a caretaker. The narcissistic parent with a stabilized self-worth can parent much better than one who is drowning in their own emotional pain.

This form of closeness is based on coercion. Neither the parent nor the child has any faith that the other will be there for them of their own accord. The parents' fear of not having the fuel they need to keep them propped up leads to them forcing the child to be their fuel. The child's fear of not having a parent forces them to comply. As this mode of closeness gets practiced it can be confused with connection. Freely chosen closeness cannot have a place in this world.

What closeness can mean now

To make the switch to empowered closeness you must have faith that important others are doing the same. You are your own fuel in your life and so are they in their lives. In this world, each person is responsible for filling and using their own gas tank but no one is alone.

This form of presence feels very different from the coercive presence of a narcissistic parent. In this world, no one is forced to be there for someone else. Part of being free to choose and pursue your own fulfillment allows you to choose to give and receive support.

This freedom allows you to conclude that the other person is there because they want to be. And if someone else is choosing to show up for you then it must be because there is something in you that is valuable. This conclusion sets one up for a very sturdy and mobile basis for self-worth. No matter how hard you push in your own direction you know you are not alone because there is something inside you that important people are drawn to.

> Jennifer had continued her trajectory after college. She took a job in a city far from her hometown. She continued to experiment with exercising her personal freedom. She nurtured the friendships where she was treated well and avoided those where she was not.
>
> At her job she found herself drawn to a coworker named Matt. He was easy to talk to. She noticed she felt relaxed around him. He seemed interested in what she had to say and got her wry sense of humor. One day Matt asked if she would like to get a coffee and she agreed. A relationship began.
>
> Jennifer found herself sharing more with Matt than she ever had before. She also wanted to know as much as she could about him. Jennifer was caught off-guard by Matt finding whatever was important to her important to

him. He would show her that he thought about her during their time apart by telling her a follow-up thought about something they had discussed in her life.

Jennifer found herself indulging in long submerged interests. She had always enjoyed drawing and began to do so after work. She half-expected Matt to lament her taking up 'yet another' hobby and be resentful. He continued to helpfully disconfirm these expectations by being excited that she had found a new interest.

All the while, Matt was contentedly pursuing his own aims in his life. He found purpose in his job and liked to talk about what he was working on. He prioritized his close friends and carved out time to spend with them. He enjoyed woodworking and would spend time after dinner on various projects.

Jennifer found herself interested in what Matt found interesting in his own life, too. She liked to check in on him in his woodworking and see what he was creating. They would discuss his projects at dinner sometimes.

As Matt and Jennifer built a life together they did so with very different bricks and mortar than what Jennifer was used to. Their relationship was built on their mutual and ongoing willingness to be there for themselves and each other. They knew that taking care of themselves did not take away from the other person. And they got to have faith in the other's continued goodwill as they pursued what they found fulfilling.

24

Heal From Narcissistic Abuse by Taking Others' Support for Granted

> *Did you work extremely hard to make your narcissistic partner or parent happy yet always seem to be falling behind?*
> *Was it especially dangerous to expect something from them?*
> *Was it impossible to assume they were going to be happy with you?*

These questions point to the pseudo-reality that a narcissistic abuser works to impose upon the person in the scapegoat role to them. In so doing, they elevate their own needs to the forefront and render the scapegoat's needs as nonexistent or offensive. One of the problems for the scapegoat is that they have no one in their corner. That is, they have no one whom they can assume cares for them and whom the scapegoat can essentially forget about or 'take for granted'.

I use the phrase 'take for granted' because I have heard many survivors of a narcissistic parent say that their parent accused them of this throughout their upbringing. They assumed they were selfish and emotionally callous for their parent to be accusing them of this. Often these survivors would work to not take the narcissistic parent for granted as they were being accused of. Here's the injustice in this scenario: a child is SUPPOSED TO be able to take a parent's love and support for granted. In fact, all relationships require some measure of taking the other person for granted. It's what allows us to use relationships in a real way. To be able to receive as well as give – not just one or the other. A narcissistic parent who weaponizes this phrase against the scapegoat child can make that child turn against their own very healthy needs to take others' for granted at times.

A narcissistic parent targets the scapegoat's efforts to take others for granted in a healthy way. In response, the scapegoat child may develop a morality and corresponding feelings of shame centered on self-deprivation. For example, the "right" thing to do for the scapegoat child is to put themselves last and failure to do this can result in feelings of shame and guilt. The narcissistic parent is actually the one taking the scapegoat child for granted without any reciprocation of the favor. The meaning of 'taking for granted' for the scapegoat survivor can change from something exploitative to a sense of healthy entitlement.

A narcissistic parent blocks the scapegoat child's healthy entitlement

In a child born to a good-enough family the expectation is that the child will expect their needs to be met. The assumption here is that the parents in such a family had their needs met well enough in childhood or did work on themselves to know they are healthily deserving of having their needs met. As a result, they want to see their child get their needs met too.

The child's self in healthy development

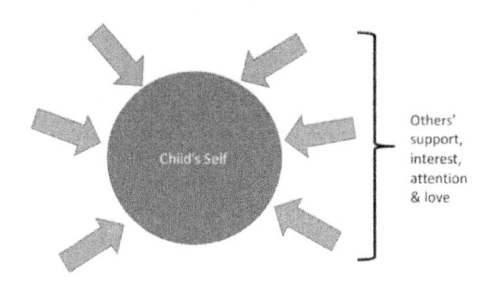

[Diagram: A blue circle labeled "Child's Self" with arrows pointing inward from all directions, labeled "Others' support, interest, attention & love"]

The child is focused on themselves and feels entitled for others to focus on them too.

The child does not have to worry about the others' interest running out or getting attacked for 'needing too much' from them.

The child lives in a world of being 'given to' without having to pay it back.

In these situations the child effectively gets to take the support from without 'for granted' so that they can focus on themselves in a very developmentally appropriate way. As a result the blue circle that is the child's self is completely theirs. They get to build and strengthen a sense of self who expects that others are available to meet their needs.

Here is what happens in adolescence:

The adolescent/adult's self in healthy development

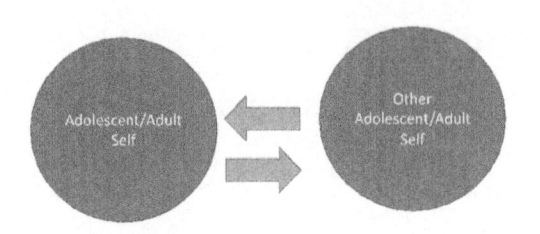

The adult/adolescent can focus on themselves and expect focus from another adult AND willingly give the same back to other adults

Between the adolescent/adult's own self and the capacity of the other, they don't have to worry about being a burden to the other

The adolescent/adult lives in a world where they take turns giving and receiving. They can take the other for granted and be taken for granted in healthy ways.

Here is what can happen for the scapegoat child's self in development:

The scapegoat child's self with a narcissistic parent

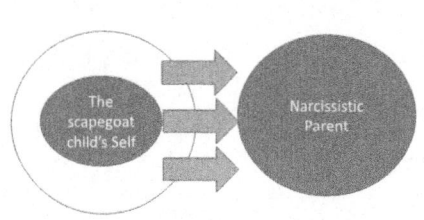

The child has to focus on the narcissistic parent MORE than themselves.

The child has less internal real estate for themselves. 'The blue territory' has shrunk.

The child has to worry about the others' interest running out or getting attacked for 'needing too much' from them.

The child lives in a world of constantly 'giving to' yet being told they don't give enough and need 'too much'.

The impact on the scapegoat child

The child now has to tend to someone else – the narcissistic parent – more than themselves. The scapegoat child gets taken for granted by the narcissistic parent but is forbidden from similarly using the parent. Now, the child must find a way to adapt to these harsh circumstances. I've found that one common way of doing this is to develop a morality on the supposed virtue of self-deprivation. So, the child has to believe that they do not deserve to have someone for them to take for granted. But this belief can be held unconsciously while consciously the virtue of self-deprivation is pursued. The child and later the adolescent and adult may constantly be scanning environments to find opportunities to help others, not take up too many resources or make any demands on others. The price of violating the code of self-deprivation can be a profound experience of shame and guilt.

This ethos of self-deprivation fits very well with what the narcissistic parent requires from the child. Namely, the parent is the only one who is allowed to get their needs met and take others for granted in doing so. The scapegoat child who disavows their own need to take the narcissistic parent for granted gets a moral reward for doing so. The scapegoat child is also spared the narcissistic parent's wrath they might otherwise encounter if they expected more from that parent.

Recover your right to take others for granted

If these circumstances resonate with you, you might wonder what you can do about it today. A lot of healing can happen in challenging and dismantling the morality built around self-deprivation for the scapegoat survivor. To establish satisfying and useful close relationships, we all need to be able to take the other for granted at times to get our needs met. It is an essential part of the trust needed in such relationships.

In good relationships, there can be a measure of turn-taking in taking the other for granted. For example, a spouse who has a problem at work may tell their partner about it after work. The spouse has to assume the partner will be interested and engaged in what they are saying. By taking their partner's interest and engagement for granted, the spouse gets to use the interaction to help them figure out how they want to address the problem at work.

But, in a narcissistically abusive relationship, the narcissist may claim that your expectation of their interest and engagement in such a situation is taking them for granted in an offensive way. Once the scapegoat survivor learns how relationships should work, they can tell a narcissistic abuser who makes accusations: "I'm trying to take you for granted because that's what people are supposed to be able to do in relationships, but you just won't let me."

To get to this point, however, it can be important to challenge the system of morality based on self-deprivation. It is critical for a scapegoat survivor to develop safe relationships to have a context to challenge these ideas. The scapegoat survivor needs to learn that someone else who matters will take the survivor's needs seriously and respect. Therapy can be a useful way to find such experiences and contrast these new experiences with the rules you had to abide by while in a relationship with a narcissistic parent or partner.

Pillar #3:

Defy the Narcissist's Rules

25

Defying The Narcissist's Rules with The Third Pillar of Recovery

> *Do you associate closeness to others with feeling less than them?*
> *Do you caveat your accomplishments so that it's really hard to feel proud of yourself?*
> *Is there an invisible but powerful pressure to feel bad inside?*

A scapegoat child knows that only the narcissistic parent gets to consciously like themselves. The child must dismiss from consciousness positive information about who they are. Doing so meets the narcissistic parent's need to feel superior. This rule disempowers the child so they do not challenge the parent's authority. All of this allows the child to stay in relationship to the parent.

The scapegoat child learns that feeling good about who they are is dangerous. It seems to offend their narcissistic parent. The child finds themselves feeling as if they have done something wrong when happy. Their parent may withdraw or grow vengeful to make the child think this. The child only feels like they are being who they are supposed to be when they feel bad about themselves. This is when they feel like their parent is there.

Scapegoat children internalize these patterns of interaction. They work to stay close to their internalized parent by acting as if that parent is still around and in charge and/or by treating themselves the way their parent did. Scapegoat survivors can stay psychologically close to their narcissistic parent by diminishing themselves. The survivor feels more distant from their internalized parent when they consider positive information about themselves. Feeling distant can lead to what I have called the three A's. The scapegoat survivor is left feeling abandoned, anguished, and astray. These painful feelings get relieved when closeness is restored. The rub is that closeness means the survivor must disapprove of themselves.

The Third Pillar of Recovery helps the scapegoat survivor to profitably defy their narcissistic parent's rules. The strategy involves allowing yourself to pursue what makes you happy, strong, and free. The critical ingredient in this pillar is seeing what happens when you do this. Do the people around you recoil or attack? If you have safe people in your life today then the answer is likely to be 'no'. Instead, they remain connected to you even when you like who you are. Experiencing this outcome helps the scapegoat survivor separate feeling good from losing needed connection.

Staying close to your internalized narcissistic parent forbids feeling good

Someone who is pathologically narcissistic has to see their opinion as more correct and important than others. They can feel worthless if they are not agreed with at all times. A scapegoat child learns that their narcissistic parent's opinion of them has to matter more than their own. This child is in the tragic position of having to not only prioritize their parent's opinion. They also have to agree with the parent's opinion that they are defective and undeserving.

This equation prevents the scapegoat child from feeling good about themselves. Being close to their parent means buying into their own - supposed - inferiority. As the child grows older, they internalize this pattern of interaction. They stay close to their internalized narcissistic parent by finding flaws in themselves and experiencing others as superior. Doing so spares them from the dreaded state of being nobody to no one. They are left with being an inferior somebody to a superior someone.

The Scapegoat Child Being an Inferior Somebody to a Superior Someone

The child remains someone to their narcissistic parent when they clap for that parent as an admiring onlooker.

clap clap

Scapegoat Child

This diagram illustrates the position the scapegoat child is put in. They are forbidden from being on the figurative medal stand. Only their narcissistic parent is allowed on. The parent is to be the recipient of the gold medal while the child looks on fondly. The payoff for the child is having their parent stay in relation to them.

Anita found it impossible to make her mother happy with her. Despite being regularly complimented by her friends and teachers, her mother never seemed pleased. From first grade onward Anita knew it was a matter of 'when' not 'if' her mother berated her for a mistake of some sort. Anita might not put her shoes in her closet as precisely straight as her mother said she should have. She would then get yelled at for her "carelessness and lack of respect" for all the things her mother did for her.

At first, Anita found her mother's tirades to be a misunderstanding. She did not put her shoes crookedly in her closet because she did not respect her mother. So, she would tell her mother as much. This did not go well. Her mother accused her of 'not listening' and grew even more enraged.

Anita learned it was futile to offer her own opinion of her motivations in these moments. The only thing she could do was let her mother berate her without interference. At some point, her mother would finish, and they could get on with life. Anita, though, had to show tacit agreement with her mother's distortions of her. She told herself that her own opinion is faulty. Her mother is the one who knows how things 'really' are and she should pay attention. She found herself prioritizing the opinion that she was a careless, thoughtless, and rude little girl.

Anita's mother was managing her own feelings of worthlessness by foisting them onto Anita. Her incessant invalidation of Anita's perspective messed with Anita's ability to internally disagree. She was left accepting internally and externally her mother's vicious character assassinations. This was how her mother got Anita to identify as the worthless one between the two of them. Her mother could feel protected from these feelings so long as she could see them in Anita instead of herself. At great cost to Anita.

Anita grew to understand that the only way to interact with her mother was to show admiration for her. Doing this, Anita realized, seemed to make her mother less hostile. To survive her childhood she had to show admiration to the same person who was consistently devaluing her.

As she grew older, Anita found herself treating herself much like her mother did. She would second-guess her own ideas. She would assume that others would find out how careless and selfish she "really" was. And she would manage to find friends and partners who treated her in a similar fashion.

Two ways scapegoat survivors prevent themselves from feeling good

The scapegoat child and survivor must evacuate reasons to like themselves. This allows them to stay close to their actual then internalized narcissistic parent. Here are two of the ways they may do this:

1) What counts is on the outside

Parents of scapegoat children like Anita insist on the child's badness. This insistence is at odds with the child's inner sense of their own basic goodness. This is confusing for the child. It is also threatening to their ability to be the person their parent "knows".

Scapegoat children may cope by telling themselves that the only thing that matters is how others judge them. They may incentivize themselves by imagining all the fanfare and love that will come when they win an approving judgment. This "carrot" makes it easier to dismiss their own judgment of themselves. Now they are less at odds with being the person their parent seems to know. They are who the parent tells them they are because it is the parent's judgment that has to count.

Anita's childhood demonstrates this coping strategy. She had no choice but to prize her mother's vicious opinion of her over her own.

2) Snatching defeat from the jaws of victory

The scapegoat child and survivor who encounters success is in danger. They now have a reason to take pride in themselves. As badly as they want this feeling, it is too threatening to embrace. Doing so would upset the order their parent insists upon. The child is to be bereft of anything worthy so the parent can be replete with it.

If the child violates this premise they are at risk of feeling abandoned, anguished and astray (i.e. the 3 A's). These are the unbearable set of feelings that emerge when the scapegoat child diverges from the inferior position. They go from feeling like the inferior child to their superior parent to feeling like nobody to no one.

The child protects themselves from the 3 A's by finding faults in themselves that supposedly negate their successes. A scapegoat survivor has been trained to assume something is wrong with what they have done. These assumptions do not have to be reasonable to be believed. Just like Anita learned not to question her mother's accusations so the scapegoat survivor does not question their self-criticism. Once they have a reason to re-establish their inferiority, they can feel close to their internalized narcissistic parent again and be spared from the 3 A's.

Don't Outshine the Master

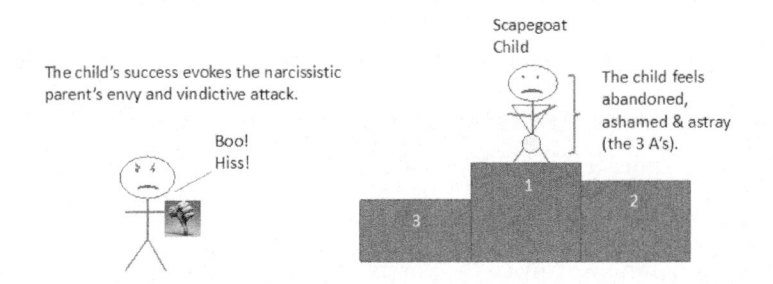

The child's success evokes the narcissistic parent's envy and vindictive attack.

Boo! Hiss!

Scapegoat Child

The child feels abandoned, ashamed & astray (the 3 A's).

This diagram is meant to capture the terrible consequences the scapegoat child faces if they get on the podium. If the child experiences success in view of the parent they are not cheered for. Instead the parent is likely to feel envious and respond with a vindictive attack. As a result the child learns to associate excelling with the 3 A's.

The third Pillar makes it safe to feel good

In conjunction with the other two pillars, living in defiance of the narcissist's rules reprograms the scapegoat survivor's mind to equate feeling good with safety. Once the survivor has applied the first two pillars they have a good understanding that their parent's narcissistic abuse was not their fault and they are treated well in their current friendships and relationships. The scapegoat survivor now has resources to combat the 3 A's that can emerge when they feel good about who they are.

Feeling good about oneself while in connection to safe others is the essence of this pillar. The specific rules the scapegoat child had to live by under their narcissistic parent can vary. However, they will be some permutation of the idea that the scapegoat child is defective and undeserving. This Pillar helps the scapegoat survivor accrue new experiences of feeling adequate and deserving while remaining cared for by the safe people in their life. Remaining cared for combats the survivor's expectation that they will face the 3 A's if they defy the narcissist's rules.

Pillar #3 Makes it Safe to Win

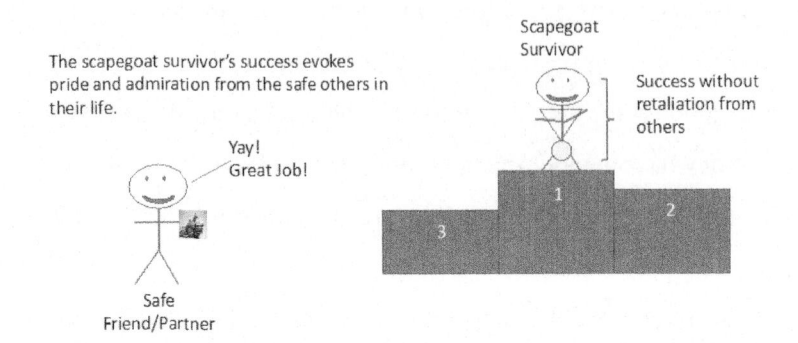

The scapegoat survivor's success evokes pride and admiration from the safe others in their life.

Yay! Great Job!

Safe Friend/Partner

Scapegoat Survivor

Success without retaliation from others

This diagram illustrates how the third Pillar of Recovery makes it safe for the scapegoat survivor to win. When the survivor finds themselves on the podium in life they are cheered for rather than attacked. Over time such experiences build the survivor's belief in new rules that allow for them to feel adequate and deserving.

26

Take Off the Scapegoat Nametag at The Narcissistic Family's Conference

> *Do you often expect rejection when in a group of people?*
> *Do you want to see yourself as equal to other group members but feel lower status?*
> *Does it feel like you are the problem, instead of the group of people putting you down?*

In a business conference the attendees are required to wear nametags and there is usually a conference agenda that lists out who is doing what and when. The most revered member of the conference usually gives the kickoff or keynote speech. Then there are other high status members who give presentations. It is a useful and harmless arrangement in the regular world.

But the narcissistic family's conference goes a little different. Here, the narcissistic parent is always giving the keynote address and the enabling family members often get to give their own presentations. But in the conference agenda of the narcissistic family there are explicit instructions for the members to treat one specific attendee very poorly. It could read like, "If you ever see _____ in the hallways or at one of the talks be sure to put them down verbally, react like what they think and feel is crazy, talk unkindly about them to other conference attendees, roll your eyes whenever they start to speak, and gang up on them with other conference attendees. You will be able to identify this person because they will have 'SG' (i.e. scapegoat) on their nametag."

Metaphor can be a powerful tool for encapsulating a false reality that has been imposed on a scapegoat survivor. I am going to use the metaphor of the narcissistic family conference and what happens when the scapegoat leaves the conference as a way to understand and envision how to defy the narcissist's rules.

The narcissistic family conference

When you walked into your house, it was likely apparent and even second-nature to be told to put on the scapegoat nametag and be ready to be mistreated in the ways the conference agenda or brochure specified. In fact, the narcissistic parent was akin to the person at the front of the conference where you must go to sign-in and be given a nametag. The scapegoat nametag was already lying there on the table and had to be given to somebody. You happen to be the person who got it. There's a real arbitrariness to what makes the child get the scapegoat nametag. It's more that the nametag exists and must be assigned than having anything to do with who the child actually is. Of course, in the confines of the conference that arbitrariness is not acknowledged. The child wearing the scapegoat nametag is assumed to deserve the designation. It's not the result of the conference organizer's psychopathology.

Leaving the conference

For the scapegoat child and survivor life can take them in directions that depart from the narcissistic family's conference. When the scapegoat survivor goes in these other directions, they may start to notice how the scapegoat nametag is only applied at the conference. At school and/or with friends they might notice being reacted to differently. They may have felt respected and not singled out in the way they routinely were at the conference. As this kind of experience accrues and the scapegoat survivor grows to experience a different world outside of the conference they begin to question the rules and regulations of their family's conference. The survivor may even seek frames of reference with other non-conference goers to get perspective on how wrong and corrupted the family conference structure actually was. As this new – and accurate – understanding gets solidified, the scapegoat survivor grows to realize the supposed identity they had at the conference was just a nametag. It was not who they actually were. At this point, the scapegoat survivor may decide never to set foot in that conference again. This is how it is useful to cultivate distance from the narcissistic family's conference. Distance prevents you from having to wear the scapegoat nametag and/or having it slapped onto you by another conference goer.

Ripping off the scapegoat nametag

As the scapegoat survivor gets distance from the narcissistic family conference they may look down and notice the nametag on their shirt. I think an important time in recovery comes when another family member metaphorically encounters the scapegoat survivor outside of the conference. That family member may try to pick up where they left off and treat the survivor like they are different, crazy, or destructive in one way or another. At this point the survivor may look down and realize that this family member still thinks the conference rules apply when the survivor knows they don't. The survivor looks down and pulls the nametag off of them, looks at the family member and just says very firmly but matter of factly that this is not how things are going to go anymore. In these moments, it's the survivor's recognition that they are not who they used to have to be that is most powerful. The survivor already possesses the power of that knowledge and is simply relaying that to the family member who still has the wrong impression about the survivor.

27

Living In the First Person After Narcissistic Abuse

> *Do you feel bossed around by other people's expectations?*
> *Do you get extremely anxious or blank when making a decision for yourself?*
> *Do you find yourself living through the eyes of others instead of your own?*

When the only viable parent is also narcissistically abusive then the child is stuck. Yes, the child wants to get away from the source of harm. But the child cannot survive if getting away leaves them parent-less.

Under such conditions the scapegoat child has to override their instinct to flee. This means finding a way to make being deprived, devalued and controlled seem tolerable. One way the scapegoat child can do this is by caring more about what the parent thinks of them than what the child thinks of themselves. Now all that matters is the parent's opinion. If the parent is unhappy with the child then the child is unhappy with themselves. If the parent is happy then so is the child.

Now the scapegoat child has a reason to stay close to a parent who is hurting them. The problem is that what makes the narcissistic parent happy is often what makes the scapegoat child suffer. And what makes this parent unhappy is the scapegoat child's growth.

The scapegoat child overrides their instinct to flee a narcissistic parent by caring more about what the parent thinks of them than what the child thinks of themselves. As adaptive as the strategy is, it later robs the scapegoat survivor of living their lives in the first person. Therapy is a way to learn that relationships no longer require you to adopt the other's mind as your own.

The threats posed by the narcissistic parent

The child in the role of scapegoat to the narcissistic parent cannot avoid them. If the other parent is emotionally unavailable and/or absent then the child must stay attached to the narcissistic parent. The child has to become wary of their own flight instinct because it leads them towards being parent-less. Being without a parent can be akin to psychic annihilation to the very young child. This can feel like an internal obliteration to be avoided at all costs.

So, the scapegoat child must find a way to psychologically stay with the parent who is hurting them. Staying involves the scapegoat child overriding the impulse to flee from harm. This is a tall psychological order.

The scapegoat child's "solution" to stay with the narcissistic parent

The scapegoat child stays attached to the narcissistic parent by adopting the parent's mind as their own. The child can reason - often unconsciously - that their parent is always right. This helps them avoid the parent's wrath for challenging the parent's authority. Furthermore, if the parent is always right, then their opinions, feelings, and thoughts are the most important.

These conclusions lead the scapegoat child to care most about what the narcissistic parent thinks of them. The child's own thoughts about themselves seem far less important. Now when the parent attacks the child's character or behavior the child "knows" they deserve it. If the parent is always right and they are devaluing the child then the child must be value-less.

This strategy has several adaptive benefits for the child. It overrides the child's flight response. The parent is no longer the source of harm. The child's "badness" is what causes the child harm. The parent is just reacting to how the child "is". Now the child wants to flee themselves for the favor of the narcissistic parent. The child is aligned with the parent against the child's self.

Hector had a narcissistic mother and emotionally remote enabler father. His mother's stance towards Hector always seemed to be: "stay close to me so I can keep hurting you." His mother regularly screamed at him for pseudo-offenses around the home. However, he could not know that this was what was happening at the time. He needed his mother too much - despite how abusive she was.

Hector had found a way to keep himself safer in the fifth grade by asking himself what his mother would want him to do. He policed himself to not do or be anything that would cause her to be upset with him. It hurt too much when she yelled at him. He had to find a way to limit it.

In middle school, Hector was confused by his mother's refusal to let him see and enjoy his friends. His efforts to convince her that he should be allowed to see them only made her more angry. He found himself reasoning that there must be something wrong with his friends. Staying home with his family was the morally right thing to do, and he was being immoral by wanting to go out.

Later in therapy he realized that his reasoning at the time was done under his mother's coercion. He saw how he had to conclude that she was right about everything. He also had to question and accuse himself when he disagreed with her. Hector felt intense grief for himself as he remembered how isolated and alone he felt throughout his adolescence. What he further mourned was that he was made to feel so alone while doing what he thought was the "right" thing.

Hector saved himself by caring more about what his mother thought about him than what he thought about himself. Caring more about her thoughts about him resulted in less disagreements with her. Fewer disagreements meant less attacks on him. The cost was having to feel like he was not in charge of himself.

5 impacts of this "solution" on the scapegoat survivor

The scapegoat child and later the survivor cannot live their lives in the first person. They have been forbidden to think and feel freely. Doing so could have led to their instinct to flee their narcissistic parent. Flight from the person one needs must be thwarted. Caring more about what the narcissistic parent thinks about the scapegoat child than what the child thinks of themselves does this.

#1: The scapegoat survivor is skeptical of their own opinions, conclusions, and feelings

For the narcissistic parent to always be right, the scapegoat child must always be wrong. The narcissistic parent acts in ways that are hypocritical, duplicitous, vindictive, and self-promoting. The scapegoat child who sees this clearly must question their perceptions. Now, they can regard the parent as always right without as much dissonance.

#2: Nobody else's positive opinion about the scapegoat survivor matters

There is not much room for opinions other than the narcissistic parent's to matter. The scapegoat child received positively by other people is in a difficult position. This feedback conflicts with their parent's view of them. Since there can be only one person who is always right -the narcissistic parent - the child must dismiss the positive feedback. They might tell themselves, "My friends don't really know me", or "These people must be messed up if they think well of me."

#3: An amoral world

This solution is a product of the narcissistic parent's coercion and the child's need for attachment. It is an arrangement premised on power rather than ethics. The child has to regard what is right as what makes someone else happy. This someone else is not bound by any moral code themselves. They will punish the child for offenses that may be ethical but are displeasing. For example, Hector recalled how his mother screamed at him the loudest when he told her not to attack his younger sister. He did something just but was punished even more for it.

#4: Boundaries become impossible

When the scapegoat survivor has to care more about what others think of them than they think about themselves, boundaries become confusing. A boundary requires an initial clear sense of who you are and who the other person is. This solution muddies such an understanding.

The scapegoat survivor can have difficulty knowing how they want to be treated. They have had to get used to living in a state of pain throughout their upbringing. They did this by thinking of themselves through their narcissistic parent's eyes. Setting boundaries means that one can safely say what they want through their own eyes.

#5: Hard to identify narcissistic abusers today

When attachment has come to mean caring more about others' views of yourself than your own then you may be vulnerable to narcissistic friends and partners. Since this strategy prizes the other's claims over your own it will be difficult to experience your feelings as valid. So, the hurt feelings you experience in these relationships are less important than what the other person claims. This is exactly the scenario faced with a narcissistic parent.

How therapy can help the scapegoat survivor live in the first person

Having to adopt this strategy reflects a severe level of narcissistic abuse. It only happens when the scapegoat child has no other option for attachment than the narcissistic parent. Insidiously, this solution can live on in the scapegoat survivor.

What is needed is a relationship that does not depend on the survivor adopting the other's mind as their own. The challenge can be that the scapegoat survivor may still experience others in this way.

Longer-term therapy where the therapist affords some neutrality can be particularly helpful. The goal of therapeutic neutrality is not to make a client feel alone or strange in their experience. Instead, it affords enough space for the client's ways of organizing their reality to come forward.

The goal of this form of therapy is for the client to get to be with themselves with someone else protectively there. This is typically a nonverbal process that takes time to develop. A different relational calculus is being introduced to the client. It is one that wholly allows them to be themselves while the therapist remains present. This may seem disorienting for a time until this new arrangement gets to be felt and appreciated.

Hector stayed in his therapy for many years. My silence at the start of treatment would initially create a lot of anxiety for him. He had trouble focusing on himself in the presence of someone else. He would get overwhelmed with a feeling of being scrutinized and criticized. It would stop his ability to think.

Hector and I traced these moments of him feeling scrutinized and criticized to him thinking critically about me. Doing so constituted a departure from the old rule of how to avoid danger - that the other person was always right. To protect himself from the wrath he anticipated he would experience himself as the one deserving criticism. My neutrality was important for this to be seen as a feature of Hector's psychology. Now that we both understood what was happening in these moments Hector felt a little more free and safe to consider his own thoughts about me.

Bit by bit the ways Hector had to prioritize his mother's perspective over his own began to give way. Hector felt it more possible to think his own thoughts in my presence. Something different and new held us together. Something that did not require Hector's obedience. With this experience under his belt he sought out relationships in his life that afforded something similar.

Ways to live in the first person outside of therapy

If therapy is not available, there are other ways to defy this rule of the narcissistic parent. You might seek out professional or personal roles that require you to express yourself. By doing so, you are putting yourself in the position of speaking from your vantage point. Here are a few examples:

- Joining a choir where you get to sing and others hear your voice.
- Joining a book club where you get to share your reflections about the book
- Resolving to share one of your ideas in each business meeting you have. The goal is not for each idea to succeed but just for you to get used to speaking up.

These types of roles can help scapegoat survivors get used to knowing what they think and sharing it with others.

28

Recovering Honesty After Narcissistic Abuse

> *Do you assume that you must keep secret what you think about others?*
> *Do you feel at fault when someone who matters to you lets you down?*
> *Do you worry about offending others if you tell them how you 'really' see them?*

The fundamental rule for the child of a narcissistic parent is to not think or speak critically of them. The narcissistic parent is beyond reproach. The problem for the child is that their parent acts in ways that offer plenty of reasons for reproach. The child must not be honest to themselves or others about their misgivings. This is the only way to stay in their parent's reality.

A parent who is not narcissistic is OK with their child seeing their fallibility. Being imperfect does not mean being worthless like it does for a narcissistic parent. Children who grow up in these families are allowed to think and speak critically of their parent. Doing so does not threaten their ability to participate in the family's reality.

The danger of honesty with a narcissistic parent

A narcissistic parent is constantly on guard against feedback that challenges their superiority. This parent may react to honest criticism with extreme hostility and contempt. Their child learns not to think or speak critically about their parent - or else!

There are two components to the 'or else' which serve as a powerful deterrent for the child. First, being someone whom their narcissistic parent will relate to means seeing the parent as flawless. If the child breaks this rule they risk being someone the parent does not "know". Going unknown to a parent can feel like being nobody to no one and must be avoided.

Second, the parent may react to challenges with extreme hostility and contempt. Their fragile self-worth depends on seeing themselves and being seen as superior. They can believe they are entitled to such treatment. A child who notices the parent's flaws is refusing to give what the parent believes they deserve. The parent may grow enraged and contemptuous at the child for this "offense". Such intense hostile reactions are scary and even traumatizing for the child and must be avoided.

How a child avoids this danger: Distortion

The narcissistic parent is not only fallible but often lets the child down. The child experiences disappointment and frustration with the parent yet cannot say this. To do so would threaten the parent's rebuke for not finding them to be perfect.

The child can avoid saying what they know by distorting their psychological vision. They can insist to themselves that their parent is how they demand to be seen: perfect. Next, the child has to deny that the parent is the source of any frustration. Most often the child will distortedly see themselves as the problem. The parent's deprivation of the care they need goes unrecognized. Instead, the child is consumed with their own - supposed - flaws. Now the only person deserving criticism is the child.

Living with such distortion creates an antagonistic and uncomfortable relationship with reality. The child knows that they cannot be honest with their parent nor themselves. So everything they experience must get filtered through the lens that says they are always wrong and their parent is always right. This lens must be used in the face of massive amounts of evidence that the parent is often wrong. Not knowing what is plain to see can create inner discomfort. Survivors of narcissistic abuse may feel a vague yet constant sense that something is not right. Like having to wear a wool undershirt at all times - it itches but there's no way to get relief.

Frank looked up to his father as a young child. He was in the military and always seemed strong, put together, smart, and capable. He also did not seem at all interested in what made Frank tick. Frank would look at his father with admiration and a stinging recognition of how far away he felt from him.

Frank's father would get easily bored with him. His father liked to run and play basketball. Frank tried to adopt these interests in hopes his father would want to spend more time with him. It did not work. Frank had to plead with his father to bring him along to the basketball court or go on a run together. His father would begrudgingly agree.

All of this led Frank to conclude that he was not good enough for his father to want to be around. Even the begrudging agreement to spend time together left Frank feeling like a worthless burden.

Another aspect of his father was that he did not take kindly to criticism. If Frank questioned his father's decisions in any way he would get a gruff, "Shut up! You're not old enough to know what you're talking about".

Over time, Frank learned to ignore how stingy his father was with his interest and support. He had to determine that there was nothing wrong with his father's reaction to him. Frank just was not worth enough for his father to want to be around. This conclusion pained Frank but prevented him from seeing any reason to criticize his father. He was left only with admiration and a free-floating feeling of worthlessness.

The costs of distortion for the child

Here are two costs to the child of having to distort what they see about their parent.

#1: Retreat from awareness

A basic requirement to live authentically is relative honesty. The child of a narcissistic parent has to sacrifice their honesty to see what they are supposed to see. Having to live with the impossibility of knowing your own truth can feel bleak and despairing.

The child and later adult may try to find alternate meaning in life. They can pour themselves into pursuits with the hope that success will bring them the inner peace they so want. If or when this proves unfruitful, they may reduce their self-awareness.

A child may do this via: sleeping more than usual, thinking ahead at all times and/or having a sense of unreality about themselves and others. These strategies are often enacted without conscious choice. They relieve the child from the agony of having a dishonest relationship with their parent.

The cost to retreating from awareness is that life becomes something to get through - not savor. The joy of the moment is nullified because they cannot address what feels off. Goals become important to structure one's experience. However, the child cannot experience any real pride when met.

#2: Not mattering to yourself

Denying what the child sees requires them to downgrade their importance. They have to believe their parents' needs matter more than their own. This can only happen if the child perceives themselves to have less inherent worth than the parent.

A child may learn to erase themselves from their own thinking. It becomes much easier for them to see and care for others rather than themselves. They have not been shown genuine and unconditional interest in what they think and feel. If their feelings do not matter to the parent, then it is easy to conclude that they themselves do not matter.

With enough practice, the child's world may consist of everyone but themselves. They cannot accurately perceive the parent who is ignoring them. They have to believe the lie that they are not worth anyone's attention. Thus, being unaware of their own presence becomes adaptive to the situation.

> *Frank's experience with his father made him extremely anxious whenever he found fault with others. If he admired someone and they let him down, he did not feel safe telling them so. He would confuse himself about whether they did anything wrong and emerge with a sense that he was really at fault.*
>
> *In eighth grade, Frank made a friend named Rick, who seemed cool and really interested in what Frank had to say. They shared a sense of humor and would make each*

other laugh a lot. One day, they were walking home from school with another friend named Matt. Matt, who could be mean, decided he wanted to pick on Frank that day. Rick, to Frank's dismay, joined in with Matt. He laughed at Matt's barbs towards Frank.

When he got home, Frank felt ashamed. However, he did not blame Rick for not having his back. He chalked it all up to his own defectiveness. Matt was just seeing him for how he really was, and Rick was finally catching on.

The next time Frank and Rick hung out, Frank felt the impulse to ask Rick why he ganged up on him. But he suppressed this and told himself that he did not deserve to question Rick. He felt lucky to be able to spend time with him.

The path to safe honesty

The good news is if the survivor can be in new relationships where being critical is welcomed then they can live a life free from distortion.

After surviving narcissistic abuse, new relationships are needed to heal. You need evidence that you no longer have to avoid criticizing those who mistreat you. Such evidence is generated in relationships with people who treat you well.

In a relationship with someone who does not need to be seen as perfect to feel acceptable, you have more freedom. If they do or do not do something that is frustrating or slightly hurtful, you get to tell them so. Their reaction may surprise those accustomed to being left or attacked for speaking up.

When a safe person is told how they have negatively impacted someone they care about, their priority will be that person's feelings. They want to be in relationships where the other person's feelings matter to them and vice versa. Thus, when the other tells them their feelings have been hurt, they will have two goals: 1) show that they understand and get the other's experience, and 2) see what they can do to repair what happened.

Frank found himself in therapy in his thirties because he felt an ongoing sense of disquiet within that he hoped could be healed.

I provided a type of monthly bill that Frank needed to submit to insurance for out-of-network reimbursement. Frank liked to get these submitted in a timely fashion so that his budget stayed on track. I provided the bill promptly each month for the first six months. Then I changed my billing process, and this resulted in Frank not getting the bill for 3 to 4 weeks after the end of the month.

The first two times this happened, Frank silently noted to himself that the bill was rather late getting to him. He felt a twinge of frustration then a ton of anxiety and vulnerability. It was enough to make him want to stay away from these feelings.

He felt a familiar process kick in where he questioned whether I was even inconveniencing him at all.

"What is my deal that I'm so insistent on getting the bill right on time?" "Maybe I'm a perfectionist and expect him to meet my demands. Maybe I'm narcissistic, and that's the problem."

Oddly enough, these thoughts reduced his anxiety. He was in the known place of blaming himself instead of holding someone else, who mattered to him, accountable.

This blame worked so well that he doubted his perception of who was creating the problem. It was no longer me for being late with the bill. Now the problem was Frank's reaction.

Frank and I continued to work for the next few months, and the bill continued to be late. At the same time, though, Frank was accruing more and more evidence that perhaps I would respond differently to his complaint than what he knew from his father.

When the bill came late a seventh time, he resolved to address it.

At the next session, his heart was pounding, his palms were sweaty, and he felt like he had a fireball in his stomach. Nonetheless, he pressed forward and said,

"Hey, I see that the monthly bills have been coming later than before. Is it possible to get them to me closer to the start of the month like before?"

Frank could not detect any signs of offense or indignation from me. Instead, I told him, "You are absolutely right. I switched to a new billing system and it has created this lateness. But that's not your problem. You should be able to take for granted that you will get these bills in a timely fashion. I apologize for that and thank you for focusing me on this topic."

Frank was dumbstruck. All the danger he thought he was walking into was nowhere to be found. Instead, I acted like Frank's complaint was a legitimate thing to express in our relationship. Over time, sequences like this helped Frank know he no longer had to hide his dissatisfactions with safe others from himself nor from them.

In short, telling a safe person what is bothering you can strengthen your relationship. With more and more of these experiences, you no longer have to hide what you see from yourself.

29

Realistic Self-Worth for Scapegoat Survivors

> *Is it hard to feel like you deserve the praise you get?*
> *Do you hold yourself to secret and perfectionistic standards?*
> *Have these standards motivated you yet felt impossible to achieve?*

Scapegoat children can hedge against feeling completely devalued. This is part of their psychological resilience. They may create secret and perfectionistic ways of feeling good about themselves. These ways are only known to the child. Their secrecy prevents them from being overtly at odds with the family's reality.

A scapegoat child has to stay a part of the family's reality and have a way to believe self-worth will be possible. This is an adaptive way to survive an abusive childhood. In adulthood, this secret and perfectionistic basis for self-worth creates problems. The scapegoat survivor can use current relationships to know it is safe to have shared and realistic standards. This recalibration of standards can produce a more solid basis for self-worth.

How the scapegoat child creates secret and perfectionistic self-worth

In my clinical work, I am struck by scapegoat survivors ability to eke out a basis for self-worth amidst the emotional abuse they grew up in. Despite being treated as if they are worthless at home, they might not give up the quest to know how they can have value.

As discussed, it is necessary for the scapegoat child to keep their self-worth out of reach. Their narcissist parent demands they be bereft of self-worth while the parent be awash in it. One way they may both motivate themselves to strive while keeping their goals unattainable is to hold exceedingly high standards for themselves. Though out of reach, these standards hold the promise of pride for the scapegoat child.

The painful result of not meeting their own standards is feeling confirmed as the worthless person the family claims they are. This can result in a tormenting cycle of pursuing perfection, falling short and feeling worthless.

The necessity of secrecy

The child's knowledge of their worth must remain secret so they stay who the parent needs them to be. If it leaks out, then the narcissistic parent will likely intensify their coercion to get the child to see themselves as worthless. This means acting with more punitive hostility or coldly withdrawing from the child.

The resulting flimsiness of the scapegoat child's self-worth

These features combine to create a very fragile and mercurial experience of self-worth for the scapegoat child. Since their standards for themselves are so high they cannot be reliably met. Their moments of feeling good about themselves can seem like pure luck and not something they can replicate. Upon experiencing success they may feel dread at the prospect of repeating this success.

Greg grew up in a family that sought to tear him down at every turn. Led by his pathologically narcissistic father, they would react with contempt and disgust at his presence. He internalized a lot of this disgust and believed that he was objectionable to others.

One trait that Greg protected was his physical aggression. He loved to play football at recess in elementary school. He was big for his age and his friends had a hard time bringing him down when he had the ball. He loved how this felt.

When he entered junior high school he was intent on joining the school's football team. Despite being verbally attacked most nights after dinner by his father, he believed in his ability to do well in this sport. Greg made the team but did not crack the starting lineup. This pained him and he felt like his family was right about him.

One day midway through the season, Greg had a breakthrough at practice. The first team running back was out sick and Greg was told to play with the first team. He knew all of his assignments and ran the ball well. He even scored a touchdown on one play. His coach remarked, "Wow Greg! I didn't know you had this in you. You are going to be starting or close to starting for the rest of your time here."

Greg was initially elated. He felt like he'd reached the top of the mountain he'd been climbing for so long. When he went home, he couldn't wait to get up to his room and reflect on his day at practice. He told no one in his family what had happened. In his room, he relived the plays he made and what it felt like when his coach told him he'd always be in the starting lineup. He felt like no one could touch this good feeling. Not even his father's barging into his room and yelling at him for not taking the trash out.

When Greg woke up the next day he felt nervous. Practice was happening later that day and he worried that he would be unable to do what he had done yesterday. He tried to reason with himself that he was the same player, but his nervousness did not go away. As the day wore on, he felt a nebulous dread on top of the nervousness. He was having an increasingly harder time imagining the practice going well.

Greg's nervousness was at a ten when he got on the field that day. He went through the warm up drills alright.

When it was time to practice plays, his coach said, "OK, Greg. Get in there with the first team. Let's see it again!". Greg felt like he had already lost something. The first play was designed for him to be pitched the ball on a sweep around the edge. The ball was hiked, and his legs felt like jello as he ran, looking for the quarterback to pitch him the ball. Now the ball was coming at him and he knew he was not going to be able to catch it. His hands landed on it but the ball fell to the ground. Just then a defender tackled him hard to the ground. Greg could not catch the pitched balls for five plays in a row. His coach asked him what was the matter and Greg shrugged. He did not know. Finally his coach told him to get on the bench and for someone else to run with the first team.

Greg's experience illustrates how he had to create a private and perfectionistic source of self-worth that felt unsustainable and fraudulent. This is what made him so nervous the day after his successful practice.

Scapegoat children and survivors like Greg are led to conclude that they are not in control of the events that lead to them feeling self-worth. This just happens to them and they have no influence over whether it will happen again. Greg felt this way when he woke up the next morning. He had nowhere inside to recognize that it was his skill and determination that drove the good day at practice. It seemed a matter of luck and he had no idea if it would strike again.

Forming a shared and realistic basis for self-worth

It may come as no surprise that the answer to this problem involves relationships with safe people today. The reason is that showing you value yourself used to threaten the relationship you needed with your parent. To it is now safe to do this, you need experience in new important relationships that argues otherwise. You are most likely to find this type of new experience with people who are safe.

The secret to building realistic self-worth: There is no secret!

How can a survivor develop self-worth? This question highlights an important principle in recovering from narcissistic abuse. We cannot just choose to think or feel differently. But we can control our choices and our actions.

What does this mean for developing self-worth today? It means that you get to choose practices that are aligned with finding and giving yourself credit. And you can perform these practices on a regular basis even if they do not lead to feeling differently. For example, you might try this exercise:

Write down three choices you made today that you could imagine feeling good about. If you cannot identify three choices you made then try this: imagine your best friend was telling you that they made the same choices you made today. Why would you tell them that they deserve credit for these choices? Now apply that logic to your choices. After writing these down, you may or may not feel more self-worth. Either outcome is fine for the purpose of this exercise. Do this before bed each night.

Here is an example:

Three choices I made today that deserve credit:
1. Getting out of bed in the morning.
2. Making myself dinner.
3. Watched a documentary that I found interesting.

You may wonder why you should go out of your way to give yourself credit if it does not change the way you feel about yourself. It may take some time before scapegoat survivors can feel pride in their usual and everyday accomplishments. It can seem too dangerous and unsupported to have such feelings. But it's possible to shift your emphasis to how you would like to choose and act today. By surrendering the hope or even inner mandate that you think and feel differently you actually stand to gain something. Though you may feel disappointment and disillusionment at first, this often gives way to a sense of freedom and being in charge of your recovery. [4]

---

[4] If you would like to learn more about this principle then you can check out my free webinar on the subject. Here is the link:
https://lp.jreidtherapy.com/the-key-to-recovery-from-narcissistic-abuse-webinar

Making your secret self-worth known to others

Showing that you valued yourself used to threaten your relationship to your parent. One way to learn to value yourself now is to create relationships with safe people.

Scapegoat survivors often wonder how to identify safe people. Here are three indicators of whether someone is safe to share your worth with:

1) **They tell or show you what they value about you.** If a friend or partner goes out of their way to emphasize what they value about you then they are likely safe.

2) **They agree with you about your reasons for valuing yourself.** This often comes in the form of telling them something you are proud of and seeing their affirming reaction.

3) **They are not threatened by your expressions of your worth.** This means that they do not slight or find fault with your reasons for valuing yourself.

These kinds of relationships can make it possible to recalibrate your standards to be more realistic. Working towards a goal can be praise-worthy just as much as reaching that goal. When you have safe relationships, then self-worth is readily endorsed and does not need to be kept secret.

30

Healing A Shame-Based Identity for Scapegoat Survivors

> *Do you live with the feeling that there is something very wrong and bad about you?*
> *Does it seem impossible to relieve this feeling?*
> *Do you manage this feeling by living in ways that let you feel temporarily better?*

A narcissistic parent acts in ways that are selfish, exploitative and cruel. If they are aware of how badly such behavior reflects upon them they need a way to deny this. They can hide this fact from themselves by treating their scapegoat child as if they are selfish, exploitative and cruel. Since the child depends on the parent for care they have no choice but to identify as the bad one.

The scapegoat child suffers immensely from this treatment. Everywhere they turn they face convincing accusations of their bad character. They live in a world where they are recoiled from. They learn to recoil from themselves.

It makes no difference that these accusations about the child are false. The narcissistic parent gets to define what is true for themselves and the child. Accuracy takes a back seat to the narcissistic parent's need to seem flawless.

For the child to find relief from this shame they would need their parent to own what they have disowned. But the parent has no reason to do this. Narcissistic parents can lack empathy, so their scapegoat child's feelings do not matter. This pattern can result in the child living from a constant sense of shame about who they are. Such shame can turn into an identity when they lose hope of ever being seen as good by their parent. Adult scapegoat survivors can learn how to excavate this ground level shame.

Hiding the narcissistic parent's sins in the scapegoat child

A narcissistic parent insists on their superiority to combat a core sense of inferiority. Part of being superior involves feeling entitled for others to reflect this back to them. They assume that their needs are more important than everyone else's. This assumption needs to stay hidden, though. If it were made plain that the parent thought they were better than others this could reflect poorly. Such a reflection could lead the parent back to the inferiority they are working so hard to escape.

The narcissistic parent hides their superiority by accusing the scapegoat child of being this way. They react to the child as if they are selfish, entitled, and exploitative. The child and other family members have difficulty disagreeing. They all assume that the parent would not react this way if the child were not so bad. With everyone's scrutiny on the scapegoat child's - supposed - bad character the narcissistic parent gets excused. In this way, the scapegoat child is made to pay for the narcissistic parent's sins.

> *Ed was the scapegoat child to a narcissistic mother who was always accusing him of being a bad guy. He was either selfish, inconsiderate, taking advantage, irresponsible or immature according to her. Throughout his childhood and adolescence he assumed all of this was true. No one else in the family took up for him when his mother yelled these things at him.*
>
> *He could not know what was really leading to these accusations in his mother. If he could here is what he might have seen:*
>
> *Ed's mother, Sylvia, was a schoolteacher. She cultivated the impression of caring deeply about her students. She felt very little however. Her inner life seemed devoid of meaning. The only times she found relief was when she felt like she was in charge of someone else. She got a surge of power that she cherished instead of*
>
> *Cracks in her caring facade began to show at work. One of the parents of her students complained that she had been too harsh with their son. Sylvia had been incessantly criticizing and undermining the child. The student's parents had called the principal who then disciplined her for this behavior.*

Sylvia's son was different. He seemed to genuinely want to help others. He did not have to make others feel bad for him to feel good like she did. This made her feel inferior and she hated him for it.

That night when Sylvia got home, Ed excitedly told her that he was going to volunteer for an organization that rehabilitated homes for families in need. He asked her if she would drive him to the construction site that coming Saturday morning. She wanted to explode at being 'shown up' once again by him.

Instead of encouraging his spiritual generosity she distorted it. With a scowl she snarled, "Oh give it up, Ed. Just stop trying to deceive everyone. You parade around here acting like a do-gooder who cares about everyone. Meanwhile you won't do the first thing I ask you to do around the house. I come home and your room is a mess. You can't even show the minimum amount of respect to me and this family but you want to be seen as a volunteer in the community? No. You're grounded this weekend and you're gonna think about this."

Ed felt like his heart had been hogtied with these accusations. He went from feeling a sense of dignity and usefulness to pure shame. Instead of being received with the warmth and pride he reasonably hoped for from his mother she stomped on him.

Sylvia buried her own sin of deceptiveness into Ed in this way. She construed his otherwise clean desire to help others by volunteering into an act of deception. Now, Ed was the deceptive one instead of her. This washed away some of the humiliation she felt from her principal's earlier admonishment.

The scapegoat child's resulting shame-based identity

The scapegoat child's resulting idea of who they are leaves them in a state of shame. To feel shame the child needs first to hope to be received by their parent in an attuned and supportive way. Instead the child is seen as a contemptible bad person. This break in what the child gets versus what they hoped for breaks their sense of connection to the parent. The child is flooded with embarrassment and self-loathing that makes them want to disappear.

To repair an experience of shame the child needs to restore connection to the parent. Unfortunately for the scapegoat child their narcissistic parent does not want to restore their connection. The parent needs the child to see themselves in the unseemly ways the parent is being. To relent on the claims that the child is bad would deny the cover the parent needs.

In the face of being denied hope of restored connection the child has to find a way to manage their shame. Tragically the scapegoat child cannot find true exoneration for their supposed 'bad character'. The shame they feel does not go anywhere. The child has to find a way to function around it. They may conclude that they are the bad person their parent accuses them of being. Now they just have to tolerate the resulting feelings of shame and find a way to live in spite of them.

The scapegoat child is denied pride in themselves. They may seek experiences that afford sensory experiences of pleasure. However, these are only rest stops along the highway of shame they are forced to travel.

> *As Ed entered his teenage years he felt like his life was getting darker and smaller. He could not know it at the time but his mother's transfer of her own malevolence into him was taking a profound toll. He did not like to think about himself anymore. Doing so would only make him shudder with disgust.*
>
> *Ed coped with this unrepaired sense of shame he felt due to his mother's abuse by narrowing his focus in life. He no longer volunteered nor pursued friendships that he enjoyed. He burrowedinto his schoolwork to get the best grades he possibly could. He stopped seeking social connections with his peers. He always felt like he had not done enough to get the grades he wanted. Under this sense of inadequacy, he would force himself to study on nights and weekends.*
>
> *Ed's strategy did result in getting good grades but he could feel no pride in this. He felt a surge of elation when he got his report card that quickly gave way to the ongoing sense of badness he had to contend with.*

> *Ed's approach to his studies reflected a way he coped with the shame his mother transferred onto him. He would push everything else in his life aside to pursue a goal that he could imagine being important to him. This gave him a sense of purpose that the ongoing shame threatened to dissolve. Nonetheless, he could not escape the overarching conviction that his character was shamefully flawed.*

Excavating shame from the scapegoat survivor's identity

The way to exhume the scapegoat survivor's shame is to restore connection to important others. A shame-based identity can influence the sufferer to socially isolate. Doing so lessens the fear of shame but does not heal it. Shame starts with undeserved rejection from important others. It can only end by finding new relationships where your participation is met with acceptance and appreciation. This kind of new experience rebuilds the bridge of connection to others that acts as a prophylactic to the experience of shame.

To that end you might think of an activity you enjoy and see what social connections you can build around it. Meetup.com is a website that has organized local social groups around nearly every activity under the sun. If you enjoy hiking, for example, you might check the website for a group that takes local hikes.

Finding a way to be social is the first step. The second and probably hardest step is taking action. Scapegoat survivors may feel an upsurge of shame as the first social outing grows closer. After all, contact with others is what used to lead to shame. The key here is to notice and accept whatever feelings arise as the social outing grows closer. You are not trying to have the 'right' feelings or thoughts in order to attend the outing. You have committed to going to the outing and get to notice whatever thoughts and feelings emerge along the way.

Another place to do this is in psychotherapy. Here is where scapegoat survivors can talk about and make sense of why they feel so ashamed to begin with. The therapist's job is to know when the client attempts to do what used to lead to shame and offer a different response.

A scapegoat survivor can use therapy to re-encode the earlier experiences that led to a shame-based identity. Now the survivor and therapist can consider what may have been happening in the world of the parent. In so doing, the child is no longer the only one accountable for their actions. The parent gets to be held accountable. The scapegoat survivor may initially feel shame as they recount these moments. If they persist, however, and feel understood by their therapist the shame can lift. Now the survivor can look back at memories where they were accused of bad character and see it as a reflection of the accuser instead of themselves.

> *Ed came to therapy in his mid-twenties because he felt like his life just was not working. He had friends, a career, hobbies and a partner but did not like himself.*

Every day came with an inner sense of unease that he felt for as long as he could remember.

Initially, Ed did not see a connection to his current struggles and how his mother treated him. I emphasized how easily his mother would distort Ed's personal qualities. This led to Ed feeling safer in bringing up some of the more painful ways he had been led to conclude he was a bad person.

He told me about the time his mother claimed he was pretending to be a good person by volunteering. As he did, he felt the familiar sense of shame come up. I encouraged him to continue.

Ed said, "When she said I was a fraud like that, I believed her. I even feel it now."

I said, "Tell me what you're feeling."

He said, "I feel like I'm dissolving inside. Right here in my solar plexus. I feel like a bad person and that there's no hope for me nor will there ever be."

I reflected, "You're in the never-ending state of shame that your mother's distortion of you created. You reasonably hoped to be helped in your efforts to volunteer. Instead, she treated you with contempt and claimed that what you thought was a good thing about you was "really" sinister. You went through something that was emotionally brutal and wholly undeserved."

Ed still felt the shame, but he registered what I said. As we continued to talk, he noticed that the sense of inner dissolution had given way to a solidity. He got his energy back, too. He said, "I feel like I just went through a tunnel, but now I'm on the other side."

31

Recovering Desire for Scapegoat Survivors of Narcissistic Abuse

Is it easier to know what you are supposed to do than what you want to do?
Does time spent having fun feel frivolous and unimportant?
Do you feel anxious or guilty whenever you enjoy yourself?

It is a simple but painful formula for the scapegoat child: feeling bad lets Mom or Dad feel good while feeling good means Mom or Dad feel bad. Mom or Dad are also aware of this and work hard to keep the child feeling bad so they can feel good.

The scapegoat child runs into problems when they find sources of happiness outside the family. If the child makes a best friend at school, excels in an activity they love, or finds a boyfriend or girlfriend they are at risk. Feeling happy interferes with how their narcissistic parent has to use them. Happiness makes it hard to look, act and feel worthless for the scapegoat child.

The cruel solution for the narcissistic parent is to take away the child's sources of happiness. This can mean forbidding the child to see their friends or partner, or sabotaging these relationships. When it comes to activities, the parent may refuse to let the child participate.

The scapegoat child learns that their desire to be happy puts them in danger. They are at risk of cherishing a person or experience and having it ripped away.

To save themselves from such harm they learn to hide their desires from their parent. If the parent does not know what makes the child happy, they cannot take it away. Tragically, though, the child has to hide this information from themselves. They are deprived of building their life around what makes them happy. The effects are a sense of numbness, inner emptiness and outer flatness. This can be addressed and changed over time in the course of therapy and I will describe how.

The problem that desire creates for the scapegoat child

At school, in their neighborhood or in activities the scapegoat child may find a positive reception. Maybe they find a best friend in their class and cannot wait to hang out with them. Maybe they excel in soccer and feel liked and valued by their teammates. Or maybe they have a teacher who takes a special interest in them and the child feels cared about. All of these experiences feel good, instill pride, and are desired by the child. When we desire an experience we want more of it.

The child's desire for more happiness outside the family interferes with the narcissistic parent's use of the child. They must strip the child of this desire to keep them feeling bad about who they are. Only then will the parent be able to use the child as a scapegoat.

3 ways the child is pressured to surrender desire

#1: Distorting the child's desire into something sinister

A child is vulnerable to their parent's moral assessment of them. It is excruciating for the child if the parent reacts to them as if they have bad character. The child is left feeling like who they are is devious, selfish, untrustworthy, or dangerous. These traits all translate to being unlovable in the child's mind.

A narcissistic parent may take advantage by construing the child's desires as sinister. For example, the child who finds friends at school may be told that they care more about being 'popular' than a part of the family. The implication is that the child is superficial and only interested in status. Or, the parent may recoil at the adolescent's interest in a romantic partner. The parent may claim they are too young to be in a relationship. The adolescent is left thinking there is something wrong with them for being interested in romantic relationships. Or, if the child loves an activity, the parent may claim this reflects a defect in them. Instead of supporting a daughter's aptitude to play lacrosse, the parent may call her a 'dumb jock' who will not get anywhere in life.

All of these distortions serve to make the scapegoat child leery of their own desires. Expressing them leads to feeling like a bad person.

#2: Active prevention of the child's pursuit of their desires

The second pressure to surrender desire is the parent's active intervention. A narcissistic parent may actively thwart access to the child's sources of happiness. The parent may put the child on restriction for minor offenses. Their goal is to keep the child apart from what makes them happy. The parent may make up reasons why the child cannot see a friend they are particularly excited about. Or they may forbid the child from participating in an activity they love doing.

#3: Having to be who the parent sees them as - or else!

The third pressure to surrender desire comes from within the child. The only way the child is psychologically recognized by the parent is if they are worthless. The child becomes someone their parent does not recognize if they believe their desires deserve to be met.

The agony of thwarted desire for the scapegoat child

The scapegoat child goes through the trauma of wanting what makes them happy only to find out they cannot have it. Moreover, it is all confusingly unfair why they are denied what they want. They may appeal to their narcissistic parent to grant them access to what or who they desire only to be met with utter refusal. No argument or plea budges the parent. The child learns with tragic certainty that they cannot have what they want.

To protect themselves from being hurt like this they can surrender desire entirely. Now, the parent has nothing to take from them. The child is left in a colorless world without deeply felt passion.

> *Sonja was the scapegoat child to a narcissistic mother. She was a sensitive, smart and enthusiastic child by temperament. Her mother felt empty and envious of those who seemed happy in their lives. This included Sonja.*
>
> *Sonja's childhood was a tragic tale of finding happiness then having it ripped away. At age 5 she was playing with dolls with her best friend, Kelly. In the middle of this, Kelly said, "Hey, let's play hide and seek!" They excitedly got up and began the game. Before they could finish Kelly's mother called and said she had to come home for dinner. Sonja had been having a great time and decided she wanted to watch TV. She completely forgot about the dolls that she had left on the floor in her bedroom.*
>
> *She was interrupted in watching a cartoon by her mother yelling her name from her bedroom. Sonja knew*

she had to spring up and go to her. Upon arriving at her bedroom she was met with her mother saying, "What is this Sonja? You just left all this on the floor as if you expect me to clean it up? You are such a selfish child! You don't think about anyone but yourself. Well, that's not how this is going to go. You are going to clean this up right now!".

The next day her mother said, "I've been thinking about it and I don't want you playing with Kelly anymore. She's a bad influence on you." Sonja felt tears well up in her eyes, and it seemed like the bottom had dropped out of her stomach. She knew there was nothing she could say or do to change her mother's mind.

After the immediate trauma of losing Kelly from her life subsided Sonja had to make sense of what had just happened. And she could not include the idea that her mother did not want her to be happy. Sonja saw her happiness and desire to be with a friend like Kelly as what led to - supposedly - betraying her mother. Sonja began avoiding friends who made her happy because she believed it could lead to more acts of "selfishness." Her mission was to get her mother to see her as a good daughter. Since her mother was threatened by Sonja's happiness this meant staying in an unhappy state. In order to do this, Sonja had to put out of awareness what she desired. She felt compelled to stay in her home and not do anything that would upset her mother.

How to recover desire

The process of recovering desire for the scapegoat survivor is incremental. They have had to sacrifice what makes up the center of most people's lives to survive. To keep having what they desired taken away would have left them too demoralized to go on. So, the challenge in recovering the right to feel and pursue what they want can initially seem very dangerous. They are trying to do what used to lead to disaster.

Scapegoat survivors need a way to feel safer when re-approaching their desires. The best source of such safety is a trustworthy relationship. If this has not been experienced before, then it may be hard to find such a thing. A way to ensure that you have a safe relationship to do this is to seek psychotherapy.

In therapy you are with someone who is allied with your efforts to recover desire. This stance counters the pressures that initially led to sacrificing desire with a narcissistic parent. Here is how:

1. Instead of construing what makes you happy into something sinister, your therapist is unconditionally supportive of you pursuing whatever it is that makes you happy. This sends the message that there is nothing wrong with what makes you happy.
2. Instead of making it harder to be happy, your therapist is there to promote and encourage your happiness. Instead of being opposed, you are collaborated with.

3. Since the therapeutic relationship goes on, when you resume the pursuit of happiness, you do not re-experience the threat of being nobody to no one. You get to be psychologically known as someone who deserves to be happy. This was not possible with your narcissistic parent.

Sonja entered therapy during her late twenties. She felt stifled in her life. Though she functioned at a high level professionally, she felt empty and lost personally. She and I grew to understand how Sonja learned to cope with her mother's hostility towards her happiness. At the same time, Sonja was trying to find out if it was indeed safer in the therapy to pursue what made herself happy.

About six months into therapy, she and a couple friends discussed going to 4-day music festival. The timing would conflict with her weekly therapy appointment. She felt her stomach drop as she imagined telling me that she wanted to go to a concert instead of attend therapy. She braced herself for me to scrutinize her motives and accuse her of avoiding what she should be doing.

She was relieved and somewhat surprised to find that I took her need to cancel that session in stride. I said, "Got it. Thanks for letting me know so far in advance. I was thinking that putting something you want for yourself ahead of your session that week could feel like a big deal? Is that the case?"

Sonja said, "Well, actually yes. I got really nervous and scared when we decided to go to the festival because I feared hurting you or making you mad. But I didn't want to just not go to the festival because the cost of that is too high for me. So, I reminded myself of how you have actually seemed to be towards me and thought I'd risk going through with it."

I said, "That all makes a lot of sense. You operating based upon what you want would have been seen as an offense by your mother. I was thinking how your decision to go to the festival could reflect knowing that you will not endanger important relationships today."

Sonja said, "I think that's true. I mean it's not 100% easy but it feels a lot more possible."

32

Heal From Fear of Persecution for Scapegoat Survivors of Narcissistic Parents

> *Do you worry about other finding out what is 'wrong with you'?*
> *Do you find yourself diagnosing yourself in problematic ways when you read about narcissism?*
> *Does it feel hazardous for someone to really know you?*

Scapegoat survivors of a narcissistic parent learn that nothing good happens when they are known. The scapegoat child is met with hostility at so many turns. To protect themselves they often have to create a public versus a private self. The public self can suffer many slings and arrows from the narcissistic abuser. Their private self is much more sacred and therefore vulnerable. They stow away their private self inside where they cannot be hurt.

Everyone has a different private versus public self. The contrast between these selves can seem more extreme for the scapegoat survivor. People without this kind of a traumatic history may have experienced certain relationships where it felt safe for their private self to be known. As a result, the difference between their private versus public self may be minimal.

As a child, the scapegoat survivor was forced to keep their private self hidden to survive their parent's abuse. Later, the survivor may feel like there is something wrong with *them* for protecting themselves like this. The survivor might wonder, "Why am I so closed off to others? Why can't I let my guard down?" These questions can feel alienating. The survivor feels blamed for doing what they had to do to survive undeserved hostility.

How the scapegoat child gets persecuted

The scapegoat child faces persecution just by being close to their narcissistic parent. The child learns that the person whom they hope to be compassionate towards them is instead hostile. The more the child expresses themselves the more ammunition the parent has to attack them with. The child has to create a public self that cannot be punctured and a private self that stays hidden from the narcissistic parent. This helps the child survive the abuse but deprives them of genuine connection to others.

> *Jeff's memories of his family were adversarial from the start. His mother always seemed to have it out for him. He felt like every time he walked into the room she was in she would find a reason to criticize him. 'Why was he slouching?' 'Did he clean up his room like she asked him to?' 'Why was he mumbling?'*

His father would gruffly concur with his wife's attitude towards Jeff. He largely ignored Jeff and would only pay him attention when he had left a mess.

Jeff was too busy fending off these painful attacks on his character to safely share who he was with his parents. If this is how they hurt him when he is not even showing himself, what sort of damage would they do if he did? Jeff found some solace in time he could spend alone. He felt relief from the threat of being hurt but painfully alone. Jeff learned to construct a public self that could weather the devaluation from his parents without feeling too hurt. His private self was under lock and key and allowed him a place to go in himself that others could not attack.

Scapegoat children like Jeff can learn they are at risk of persecution when around others. The only time they are safe is when they are alone.

How the scapegoat survivor protects from further persecution

Scapegoat survivors may avoid letting others get to know them. The process of being known can be associated with persecution. They may caveat their relationships and friendships to convince themselves they are not *really* close. They may tell themselves that their friends only accept them because they hide what is despicable about themselves.

Survivors may also fear being labeled as pathological by people in the mental health field. Of course this is not entirely without basis, unfortunately. However, the scapegoat survivor may find it inevitable that someone else will condemn them as mentally ill if they reveal themselves. After all, they have been in an environment where other people were always finding something wrong with them. Why would a mental health professional be any different?

> *Jeff started therapy in his mid-twenties and was prepared to be told that he was a narcissist. He told me that he finds it hard to think about others' feelings. He said that he was very self-centered. I held off on agreeing with Jeff's ideas about himself. As a more trusting relationship was built between us, we understood why Jeff was so adamant that he was narcissistic at the start of treatment. He thought it was only a matter of time before I stated what was wrong with him, so he might as well beat me to the punch.*

The good news is that most therapists seek to be allies with their clients. Their goal is for the client to feel like they are on their side. This may seem understandably doubtful for scapegoat survivors but worth discovering.

The dilemma of healing

The scapegoat survivor faces a profound dilemma as they start to heal. The source of healing will ultimately reside in finding it safe to know and be known by someone else. And being known is precisely what led to persecution in early important relationships.

In my professional and personal experience the solution is for the scapegoat survivor to allow themselves to be known on their own terms and timeline. That is, they are not being open because they must but because they want to. In order for this to happen they need to participate in a relationship where the other person displays patience and acceptance. The survivor needs to know that they do not have to rush themselves for the sake of someone else. They also need to know that the other's acceptance of them does not hinge on sharing more of themselves. They are already accepted.

With this acceptance in place, the scapegoat survivor can consider what they want for themselves. If they are safe in the relationship either way, then opening up may take on a new meaning. The scapegoat survivor may consider it plausible that allowing themselves to be known could help them. If the other's presence is truly kind and accepting, then this becomes possible.

> *Jeff continued in therapy for several years. I was consistent in my positive regard towards Jeff. I was also undemanding. Jeff was free to talk about or not talk about whatever he wanted. My interest in him did not waver either way.*
>
> *It took Jeff a long time to get used to this calm in a relationship. He was so used to the other shoe dropping where he would be attacked. Over time, Jeff's nervous*

system began to relax more around me. He felt less of a ball in his stomach telling him to flee or tense up for protection.

Jeff's initial efforts to consider that I felt safe made him feel like he must submit. Jeff's only experience with kindness from his mother was when she had a use for him. Initially, for him to let my kindness in, he assumed he had to become however I wanted. Jeff described feeling a loss of agency and ability to choose inside. He explained, "When I feel like things are going well between us in here I feel like I have to be your servant." It was important for Jeff to notice and say this in the treatment. Over the course of a year, he found it safer to see me as a kind person without handing over his independence.

The process of noticing what is happening as feelings of closeness arose in the treatment was part of what proved helpful to Jeff. He could express his conflict of wanting to feel close without feeling oppressed and be understood. I would not shift my stance of positive regard towards him. With many repetitions of this, scapegoat survivors can find it safe to assume the other person could be happy for them, not because of them.

33

The Challenge of Creativity for Scapegoat Survivors of Narcissistic Parents

> *Do you want to express yourself creatively but find it hard to actually do so?*
> *Do you grow anxious and fearful when you try to create?*
> *Do you criticize your creative work so much that it makes you not want to continue?*

To be creative is to access the core of who we are. Creating comes from within. It can feel like putting your stamp on the world saying, "this is something original that came from me." For some the need to create can feel like a demand that must be met to be at peace.

Scapegoat children to a narcissistic parent are often forbidden from being creative. They must deny the creative impulses that could lead to a demonstration of worth in the world. The scapegoat child does not do this consciously. They are convinced that they have nothing of value to creatively express.

Denying the value of their creativity solves the scapegoat child's problem of staying in relationship to their narcissistic parent but creates other problems. The scapegoat child and survivor learns to associate being creative with three punishments. The first punishment is their parent's vindictive attack for "showing off". The second punishment is feeling like nobody to no one. The third punishment is feeling psychologically lost because creativity does not seem like a real part of their identity. To recover, the scapegoat survivor needs to turn inward towards their creative impulses. They also need to be in relationships that support this part of themselves.

The dilemma of the creative scapegoat survivor

Someone with a desire to create can feel like a part of them is missing if they cannot do so. A creative person relates to the world as a canvas that they want to populate with their creations. To be prevented from doing this is to feel stifled from realizing an essential part of oneself.

The creative scapegoat child and survivor have to live in this stifled way. Their narcissistic parent insists that they operate as though they have no value. Being creative demonstrates worth and this severely strains their relationship to the parent.

> *Alina loved visual art for as long as she could remember. Her eye would naturally wonder to pictures in her environment. These pictures would swim in her mind as she would modify them in the ways she wanted. Once she had the perfect picture in her mind she had to draw it.*

Alina's father seemed to stand in her way no matter what she did. If he saw her doing something that felt meaningful to her, he would interfere. He saw the world through the lens of asking how he could turn a situation to his advantage. One way he felt advantaged was to see others frustrated or defeated, while he did not feel these ways. This made him feel superior and was very gratifying to him. Alina's father's opinion seemed to be the only one that mattered in their home. Her mother tip-toe'd around him and did not show much interest in Alina.

His approach to life tragically extended to Alina's drawing. When she was drawing her father came into the room and pulled the paper from her.

"What is this supposed to look like?" he'd sneer.

"A frog sitting on a Lilypad," Alina said.

"Hmph. If you say so," he said, as he dropped the paper to Alina and walked out of the room.

Alina felt like her energy had dissipated. She felt weighed down and still. It seemed impossible to do anything, let alone continue drawing. After a few minutes of this freeze response, she came to. Her desire to draw was absent, though. She just felt like going to her room and trying to fall asleep.

In this episode Alina's zeal to draw seemed to threaten her father. Her fulfillment could have evoked his envy or punctured his ability to see her as inferior. As episodes like this continued in her childhood she eventually stopped drawing. She would still have the pictures come to her mind. She would tolerate and try to numb the pain of not being able to get these pictures onto paper as she wanted. Over time, the pain of not drawing lessened but so did her ability to feel much at all.

3 punishments for the scapegoat child's creativity

The scapegoat child faces three punishments if they demonstrate their creativity.

#1: Attack

he child's passion for their creative pursuits may remind the narcissistic parent of their own lack of passion. This can trigger the parent's envy of the child. The parent can solve this painful state by spoiling the child's passion to create. They may humiliate the child for attempting to be creative. As the child grows deflated the parent is spared further envy. Now the child no longer seems to have what the parent lacks.

#2: Being nobody to no one

The only identity available to the scapegoat child is one of being defective and undeserving. Being creative does not go along with this identity. The child can feel at grave psychological risk if they deviate from the way their parent knows them. This is true even when the parent knows them in a way that is false and devaluing. It is always better to be a devalued somebody to a superior someone than nobody to no one.

#3: Getting lost

A scapegoat child did not have their creative attributes noticed and affirmed by their parent. As such, they may feel fraudulent and like an impostor when they try to be creative.

To feel like our traits are real we need them to be seen as real by people closest to us. The merit of the scapegoat child's creative talent is wholly denied. If the child's creativity is not recognized as a true quality by the parent then how can it seem real to the child? What does get recognized in the family are the child's - supposed - flaws and mistakes.

Scapegoat children and survivors may feel a wordless dread about proceeding with their creative gifts. Some of this danger may reflect the person venturing into psychological territory that has not been recognized as a part of who they are. Leaving who you know yourself to be - even if it is a suffering-filled identity - can feel like a psychological death.

Alina willed herself away from creative outlets in her life. She did not sign up for art classes to avoid her father's derision. She poured herself into the subjects he did not have qualms with: math and science. As a scientist himself, he regarded this type of work as worthwhile. Alina did not find this subject as compelling as drawing but forced herself to study it.

She majored in accounting in college and took a job at a firm upon graduating. Deep inside she still felt stifled and as though she was not allowed to live the way she wanted. She had moved to a different town after college and saw her father only on holidays now. One night after work she heard an ad on a podcast for therapy that got her thinking,

"Maybe I should go talk to someone. I don't feel good, I know that. Maybe counseling could help."

One of the questions on the forms she had to fill out for me asked her how satisfied she was in her current occupation. She surprised herself with her honesty and selected 'not at all'. In the first session, I inquired:

"I saw that you're not satisfied with your current work as an accountant. Can you tell me a little more?"

Alina said, "Yeah, well I just don't get any joy from accounting."

I asked, "Why do you do it then?"

Alina said, "Well, it feels like I'm not supposed to enjoy what I do. Like the way I know I'm doing legitimate work is if I don't enjoy it."

"I see," I said. "If this rule were not in place and legitimate work could be anything, what do you think you'd choose to do?"

"Drawing - no question" Alina blurted out. She felt a surge of relief and terror as she said this.

From this moment on, Alina and I would focus on what it was like for her re-engage in drawing as a part of her life. Alina wanted to devote 30 minutes per night to drawing. As she tried to do this, she registered feeling scared. She was not sure why, but she knew that the fear grew the more she drew. The only way to relieve it was to distract herself from drawing.

If she strung together three nights of successfully drawing, something else would sweep over her. She would feel a vague but powerful block from drawing a fourth night in a row. She would question whether she liked drawing as much as she thought. But she also felt like these thoughts were a means to the end of getting her to stop her momentum.

When Alina finished a drawing she often would not know what to do with herself. None of her friends or *coworkers knew that she liked to draw. She and I grew to understand why she kept this part of herself secret. She never saw herself as an artist.* To be creating art like she was while having no sense that this was part of her identity felt disconcerting. *She knew herself to be someone who struggled in life. Doing what she loved and finding fulfillment did not fit what she knew. Alina would feel lost as she reintroduced drawing into her life and self-concept.*

How scapegoat survivors can find it safe to be creative

The scapegoat child had to turn down the volume on their creative impulses and turn up the volume on their parent's messages that they were defective. In order to find it safe to be creative the scapegoat survivor needs to first rediscover those creative impulses. This process involves turning away from their parent's loud, harmful messages. Next, they must turn inward towards their own creative voice. Turning inward used to mean risking the three punishments I described earlier. As the survivor discovers that these punishments no longer occur they can feel safer to turn up the volume on their creative impulses.

The process of turning inward can feel fraught. The scapegoat survivor has had to deny that they possess value internally for so long. The result can be a belief that they are empty inside. And it may even feel this way upon first turning towards oneself.

Here is where therapy can be helpful. In an ongoing therapy you get the experience of someone being there when you pay attention to yourself. Not just a warm body but an empathic mind that is interested and supportive of you feeling connected to what is within. This type of presence counters the three punishments experienced with a narcissistic parent. You get to see that you are not attacked, you are recognized and your creativity is positively responded to.

> Over a few years in therapy Alina made more room for creativity in her life and identity. First, by talking with me about her desire to draw, we were acknowledging this as a valid aspect of her. Now, the problem was not that her creative impulses arose. It was that the three feared punishments interfered with her embracing them.
>
> My continued benign interest in what mattered to Alina helped counter the fear of attack. Gradually, Alina learned that she did not have to hide her creativity to prevent me from attacking her, which helped her feel less anxious when she sat down to draw.
>
> Alina was able to take in my view of her, too. She knew that I saw her as a decent, creative, and resilient person. This was evident in how I treated her and responded to her. Now, when Alina exercised her creativity, she could still feel like she was someone to somebody.
>
> Alina used my affirmation of her creative expressions to feel more real when she created. Over time, her passion

for drawing felt like an activity that helped her feel more—instead of less—like herself. She no longer felt lost when she was creative.

Finding creative outlets

It can be helpful for scapegoat survivors to find reliable groups of people with whom to explore their creativity. For example, if you are interested in writing, then joining a writer's group might combat what it used to mean to being creative. You are no longer alone. You are amongst people who are trying to be creative too. You are not punished for what you create. Survivors can learn that being creative does not have to be dangerous anymore. This learning may happen faster when you can be creative with others rather than alone.

34

Defy The Narcissistic Rule That Love Means Being Helped Up

> *Are you often treated as if you are a problem that needs fixing?*
> *Does it feel necessary to constantly express gratitude for others' 'help'?*
> *Does it feel scary to show off your strengths in close relationships?*

Some survivors of a narcissistic parent have learned to equate love with being helped up from the ground. The child's narcissistic parent withholds the emotional nourishment the child needs. They also visit harm on the child by making them feel the worthlessness that they themselves cannot bear. The child's needs to feel loved and safe go chronically unmet.

Against the backdrop of such a dire situation the child has to find a way to get just enough of what they need. They may notice how their parent becomes kind when they are in need of help. They now have an alternative to the ongoing pain of their parent's emotional abandonment and attacks. They simply think of themselves as deficient and in need of their parent to be complete. Operating this way brings forth something much better than being ignored or despised. It is just not an option for the child to feel loved and protected while being self-sufficient. They have to be helped off the figurative ground to get any sense of goodwill from their narcissistic parent. Needing help can become a survival-based habit.

The scapegoat child of a narcissistic parent may learn to equate love with being helped off the ground. There can be lasting impacts of this strategy on the survivor's relationship with others and themselves. However, survivors can find it safe to feel empowered and close to others in relationships where help is exchanged not only received.

When a parent can't stand their own imperfection

Many pathologically narcissistic parents can only accept themselves in a state of perfection. The parent needs a way to see others as imperfect instead of themselves.

A narcissistic parent may exploit their child's dependency on them to do this. Such parents unconsciously disavow their own imperfections and become hyper-aware of their child's supposed 'flaws'. They only recognize their child as someone who is deficient. By contrast the parent sees themselves as perfect.

One way this transfer of imperfection takes place is by only being responsive to the child when they need the parent's help. If the child presents themselves in need of help, then the parent may feel protected from their own fear of being imperfect. It is the child who is "obviously" imperfect because they need help - not the parent. With the parents' fear quelled, they can be considerate and even generous towards the child.

> Nicole's father always seemed occupied with something other than the people in his family. He had a never-ending list of chores to do around the house. Nicole's early efforts to get her father to play with her were dismissed harshly by him.
>
> She remembers having to stifle her happiness around him. She couldn't put her finger on why, but she knew not to smile or get excited around him. When her father talked to her, he expected her rapt attention. So, she had to be serious, interested in him, and mute about herself.
>
> Nicole was eight years old when she sprained her ankle while playing in the backyard. She came limping into the house and her father came to her. "Are you okay?" he asked.
>
> She was startled by his caring response. "Um, no. I hurt my ankle I think." He picked her up in his arms and put her on the couch. He gently looked took her shoe and sock off to look at her ankle. He said, "It looks like a sprain. Just lay here while I call the doctor and get you something cold to drink."
>
> Nicole was dumbfounded. Why was he being so nice to her? This had never happened before. She could not figure it out but she knew she wanted more of it.

> *When Nicole brought home an 'A' in school her father would ask her why it wasn't an A+? But if she were struggling with a math problem and could ask for his help he would readily provide it. Nicole learned, "Dad is nice when I'm struggling". So if she could find reasons to struggle then he would be kinder to her. This rule lessened the pain of feeling ignored by him. However, it curtailed her ability to enjoy her strengths and self-sufficiency.*

The child's (lack of) options

The child in this position has to take the blame for their parent's offenses. The offense in this case is not being perfect.

The child learns that the conditions of being recognized by their parent is that they be in need of help. Their other options are to be vindictively attacked or emotionally abandoned if they show their prowess. So, the child has to forge beliefs about themselves that facilitate their needing help. Beliefs such as "I am defective" in one way or another can do this.

The child who believes they are defective will have a much easier time seeking help from those who are - supposedly - effective. This belief is reinforced by the narcissistic parent's relative kindness when they ask for help. I say 'relative' because the absence of attack or withdrawal can seem like a kindness to the abused child.

A pseudo-harmony develops between the scapegoat child and narcissistic parent. The parent is full of bonhomie when the child is looking up to them for assistance, wisdom, etc. Things may go really bad when the child wants to make their own decision or exercise a strength. So it is a very uneasy calm that gets maintained at the cost of the child's ability to experience themselves as formidable.

Impacts of having to equate love with help on the child

Having to be in continual need of help wreaks havoc on the child's self-worth and independence. The child essentially learns that only one person can be upright in a relationship. And that person has to be the other person. The child finds that being self-sufficient means having no relationship to the other. As a child, having no relationship to a parent is not survivable and must be avoided at all costs.

Later, the adult survivor may continue the practice of seeming in need of help in important relationships. It can feel dangerous not to do this. Here are three ways this can show up in the adult survivor's life:

#1: Being self-critical in important relationships

Since the adult survivor learned that harmony is only possible when they are in need of the other's help, they may feel uneasy when a friend or partner encourages their strength. A good friend who commends the survivor for an accomplishment can make the person anxious. They value the relationship to this friend yet they are being held up instead of down. That has always spelled trouble in their early experience. So the survivor may go out of their way to criticize themselves and ask for the friend's advice for how to improve.

#2: Only sharing what is going wrong with important others

The survivor can learn that they can only safely share what is going wrong in life. Sharing their triumphs has resulted in attack or withdrawal in the past. This can become so practiced that the survivor may only be aware of what is going wrong. It can feel too dangerous to acknowledge what is going right in their lives.

#3: Feeling less effective than friends and partners

All of these maneuvers imply that the scapegoat survivor is less together than the other person. Of course, that is by design given the early demands of their narcissistic parent. The scapegoat survivor may feel inherently less capable than their friend or partner. This creates a disparity in worth that feels necessary but humiliating for the scapegoat survivor.

These three phenomena may lead to relationships with people who are gratified by the survivor's needs for help. The survivor's belief of being defective can make it easy to get along with such people.

Nicole got into therapy in her early thirties because she experienced anxiety most of the time. She felt particularly anxious at her job and with her friends or partner. I asked why and she explained, "I'm always worried that I'm going to say the wrong thing. I try to listen to them and ask questions but I never feel like I do a good enough job."

In the third month of therapy, I asked Nicole what made her particularly anxious at her job. She said, "Well, it's similar to with my friends, I'm always worried I'm going to say the wrong thing or not listen closely enough to them." Nicole would find herself asking her manager questions even about tasks she knew how to do. When her manager answered, she felt some of her anxiety go down.

By this time I had a sense of who Nicole was and how others experienced her. She was very perceptive, intelligent, strategic and articulate. It was hard to imagine others taking offense at her speaking up. It was clear that this worry of hers functioned to stifle her and put her in a state of needing answers she - supposedly - did not have. I shared this with Nicole and she found it hard to believe at first. I asked if she had any idea why it might feel dangerous to speak up to share what she knew.

She said, "I don't know. I would think that they would see me as rubbing their faces in what I knew that they didn't. Or I might think I know something and they *would tell me how wrong I am. It feels really scary to do."*

Nicole experienced anxiety from going along with her belief that she was defective. This belief was painful for her but had allowed her to eke out a relationship with her narcissistic father. She now got anxious when she was on the verge of showing her self-sufficiency. The anxiety would thwart her by disrupting her thinking and leave her in a state of 'not knowing'. This would allow others to occupy the status of teacher and her the student.

Moving from needing to exchanging help

If you had to habitually get on the ground to be helped up by a narcissistic parent then you may wonder what other options exist. As you leave the confines of this hierarchical relationship you can pursue reciprocal connections.

In a reciprocal friendship or romantic relationship neither person has to always be on the ground. Sometimes a person may be challenged and need support. At other times they may be succeeding and need to be celebrated. And so on. In these sorts of healthy and rich arrangements you do not feel mandated to stay in one state.

Each person can trade positions as the need arises. One day you may need compassion from your friend for the loss of a beloved pet. The next your friend may need compassion for how they were mistreated at work. Help is exchanged between you and the other.

This exchange creates mutual respect and prevents either party from feeling more powerful than the other.

This is easier said than done for the survivor of narcissistic abuse. The narcissistic parent did not allow the child to expect reciprocity and mutual respect. The parent was - supposedly - the only one who deserved respect. If the child entertained such expectations for themselves, they risked being someone the parent could not recognize. They risked being nobody to no one.

To enter into a healthy relationship where you get to exchange respect is to practice what used to be very dangerous. As a result, you can experience some of the fear and anxiety that used to accompany such practices. These painful feelings may arise in a post-traumatic fashion. That is, the danger today is objectively less than what it was in the past yet your subjective reality says otherwise.

To grow convinced that you are safe to expect reciprocity in relationships you need repeated experience of the sort. Therapy and support groups are important first steps to find this kind of experience. In both contexts you are encouraged to express yourself while not getting pathologized. Your therapist and fellow group members do not require you to be in need of their help for them to feel OK about themselves. In group, especially, you see and hear others expressing themselves in similar fashion. In therapy, you can understand why deviating from the position of needing help in relationships feels so scary. Feeling understood generally leads to feeling less alone which often leads to feeling less scared.

In the third year of therapy, Nicole got into a relationship with a man who was very interested in her. He told her how much he admired her in various ways. This did not make Nicole as anxious as it may have before she got into therapy. When she felt uncomfortable with her boyfriend's positive attention she told herself not to run from him or her feelings. She reminded herself that her sense of unease was from what she had to do to avoid the danger of having no relationship with her father earlier in life. These responses to herself helped her persevere. As time wore on she even grew to enjoy her boyfriend's admiration.

In her therapy session she said, "It is so different now. I don't feel like I have to compromise myself to be close to someone. Being close before always felt so tense. I didn't feel like the other person would be there for me unless I made them feel good about themselves. But my boyfriend doesn't seem to need that from me. He seems pretty happy with himself and pretty happy with me."

35

How the Scapegoat Survivor Can Recover Faith in Themselves

> *Do you have difficult feelings inside that seem impossible to do anything about?*
> *Have you felt adversarial towards these feelings because they are so disruptive?*
> *Is it much easier to offer compassion to others than yourself?*

Scapegoat children find themselves being devalued, deprived and controlled by their narcissistic parent. And they must attach to that parent anyway. To do this, they must find a way to not let their painful feelings get in the way.

There is a form of therapy called Internal Family Systems (IFS), that offers a helpful understanding for how the scapegoat child does this (Schwartz & Sweezy, 2019). In the IFS model everyone is understood to have multiple parts to themselves. We also have a central self that seeks to coordinate respectful and loving interactions between these parts. Healing consists of understanding how one's parts are currently configured, why they've had to do so, and patiently, faithfully, and lovingly developing a place for all the parts under the coordination of the central Self.

The scapegoat child often has to configure their parts to survive narcissistic abuse. The child sends the part of themselves that felt devalued, deprived and controlled into exile. With therapy and work within the scapegoat survivor can cultivate an attitude of faith, patience and love towards this part. The goal is to increase the sense of belongingness to all of your inner experience.

How the scapegoat child uses their parts to fit in

We all have different parts or recurring states that serve different purposes. When we need to feel close to someone we become gentle and affectionate. When we want to assert ourselves we become energized. When we want to play with others we seek what surprises and delights. All of these different parts map to the different motivational systems that make up our personality.

When a child is in a good-enough family each of these parts gets to serve a purpose that furthers the child's growth. The child's care about the feelings of others helps them develop friendships. The child's natural assertiveness is channeled towards playing sports. The child's parents tend to notice, appreciate and support these different parts. The child develops a similar inner attitude towards these parts.

The scapegoat child must burden their parts with fitting into the narcissistic parent's reality. The child's natural empathy cannot be used to further the child's growth. It must be commandeered into being alert to and meeting the emotional needs of their parent. The child's assertive part contradicts the lower status conferred upon them by the narcissistic parent. This part has to be redirected back at the child. The child's assertive part morphs into an inner critic. Now there is a place for this assertive energy to go. Now the child can still share in the parent's reality as someone who thinks of themselves as flawed.

Jamal never felt loved by his narcissistic mother. She would insist on telling him she loved him all the time and expected him to say it back to her. However, she reacted to any expression of what Jamal needed with eye-rolling exasperation. She showed outright favoritism towards his sister - seemingly demonstrating her ability to love her but not him. In her rageful attacks on him she would "offend from the victim position". He had done or not done something so horrendous that she had no choice but to yell at him.

Later in his twenties, Jamal had difficulty recalling his experience in childhood. As we worked together in therapy, I grew to understand that he had to force himself into his mother's reality. He described an inner world that felt chaotic and sometimes incoherent:

"At work I feel like my head has to be on a swivel. My boss or a coworker is going to come along at any moment and tell me I'm doing something wrong. I'm always trying to guess what it is and make sure I do things right. I get good performance reviews but I feel drained and empty at the end of every day. I usually just

go home and watch TV with a drink in my hand. There's a real empty and lonely feeling that tends to set in as I'm trying to get to sleep. I don't know what to do with it so I just force myself to go to sleep so I won't have to keep feeling it. Then I get up the next day and do it all over again."

Jamal was at a loss for how to manage these disparate states. They seemed to take him over depending on his situation. At work he had to manage others' expectations of him at all times. At home the only soothing he could find was through the numbing effects of alcohol and television. Before bed, he was visited by a seeming intractable emptiness and aloneness.

An IFS map of jamal's inner world

Jamal's inner experience corresponded to how he had to adapt to his loveless childhood. He always knew that there was nobody in his family to offer him comfort. That was not part of the reality he could share with his narcissistic mother. He felt abandoned and worthless but these feelings became a liability. Expressing the pain he felt to those inflicting it upon him did not help. Jamal had to burden the part of him that felt his feelings with staying silent. Then he had to exile this part into his unconscious. I will call this part the "hurt truth-teller".

With the hurt truth teller in exile, the "solver" part gained much more influence. This part knew the dire situation Jamal faced. With endless energy this part was always looking around for signs of trouble. Trouble could mean the slightest indication of dissatisfaction by his mother. When detected, he would spring into action to smooth out the situation. The solver part helped Jamal share in his parent's reality too. This part did not question what Jamal was responsible for or not. When the solver was told of - or accused of being - a problem, he went to work.

There was a third part that afforded Jamal some momentary relief from the rigors of his life. This part that I called the "soother" would find ways to escape by numbing his senses. When he was younger the soother would emerge as Jamal lost himself in video games alone in his room. Today the soother used television and alcohol to give him an oasis of rest from all of his inner tumult. When the soother was in charge the hurt truth teller seemed light years away. And the solver could be deactivated because Jamal was too numb to worry about signs of trouble.

Distinguishing the parts from their burdens

One of the essential processes in healing from an IFS perspective is making compassionate contact with one's parts. An important principle in this compassion is that the parts are not their burdens. Jamal's parts had been burdened with holding pain for which there was no solution, solving problems that were not his own, and dosing himself with enough relief that he could keep going. If he had a good-enough parent then the "hurt truth teller" could have just been the "truth teller". The "solver" could have been used to solve problems that he found interesting. And the "soother" could have sought relaxation in connected relationships.

At the start of therapy Jamal tended to regard his solver part as undignified and his soother as evidence of his laziness. I would counter Jamal's attitude with curiosity about each part's experience. Next, I would try to ask him how each part might be trying to help or protect him?

Over the course of several years in treatment, Jamal's attitude towards his parts shifted. His experience of the non-judgmental, curious, and compassionate attitude towards him and his parts seemed to get internalized. As this happened, something else emerged: hope.

"I've never seen the point of staying in consistent contact with myself. Life only used to feel live-able when I was not paying attention to my inner experience. Now, when I feel the pain of the truth-teller, I don't see it as endless. I know that this part deserves patience and to be listened to. And I have faith that if I do, then this part's pain can be helped. I never used to have hope for my parts before."

Jamal described an important shift that can happen in therapy for scapegoat survivors. In order for the scapegoat child to fit into the parent's reality they have to exile parts of themselves that do not fit. The child cannot keep in consistent contact with themselves. They find it hopeless to do so while dependent on the narcissistic parent. Therapy offered a relationship that did not require Jamal to exile parts of himself to share a reality with me. This allowed him to exercise patience and hope towards his parts.

Now Jamal found himself more curious than dismissive towards his hurt truthteller part. Although this part felt immense despair at having to be in exile for so long, Jamal still wanted to hear from him. Jamal also developed a hope or faith that the hurt truthteller part may not always feel this way. That with enough ongoing connection the part's hurt might heal. This hope made Jamal stay oriented towards his inner world as the path towards purpose rather than finding relief by escaping himself.

References

Afek, O. (2018) The Split Narcissist: The Grandiose Self versus the Inferior Self. Psychoanalytic Psychology 35:231-236

Azizli, N., Atkinson, B.E., Baughman, H.M., Chin, K., Vernon, P.A., Harris, E., & Veselka, L. (2016). Lies and crimes: Dark Triad, misconduct, and high-stakes deception. *Personality and Individual Differences*, 89, 34–39. doi: 10.1016/j.paid.2015.09.034

Back, M. D., Küfner, A. C., Dufner, M., Gerlach, T. M., Rauthmann, J. F., & Denissen, J. J. (2013). Narcissistic admiration and rivalry: disentangling the bright and dark sides of narcissism. Journal of personality and social psychology, 105(6), 1013.

Baughman, H.M., Jonason, P.K., Lyons, M., & Vernon, P.A. (2014). Liar liar pants on fire: Cheater strategies linked to the Dark Triad. *Personality and Individual Differences*, 71, 35–38. doi: 10.1016/j.paid.2014.07.019

Celani, D. (2011). *Leaving home: The art of separating from your difficult family*. Columbia University Press.

Diamond, D., & Meehan, K. B. (2013). Attachment and object relations in patients with narcissistic personality disorder:

Implications for therapeutic process and outcome. Journal of Clinical Psychology, 69(11), 1148-1159.

Engel, L., & Ferguson, T. (2004). *Imaginary crimes: Why we punish ourselves and how to stop.* iUniverse.

Grapsas, S., Brummelman, E., Back, M. D., & Denissen, J. J. A. (2020). The "why" and "how" of narcissism: A process model of narcissistic status pursuit. Perspectives on Psychological Science, 15(1), 150-172. https://doi.org/10.1177/1745691619873350

Jonason, P.K., Lyons, M., Baughman, H.M., & Vernon, P.A. (2014). What a tangled web we weave: The Dark Triad traits and deception. *Personality and Individual Differences,* 70, 117-119. doi: 10.1016/j.paid.2014.06.038

Krizan, Z., & Herlache, A. D. (2018). The narcissism spectrum model: A synthetic view of narcissistic personality. Personality and Social Psychology Review, 22(1), 3-31. https://doi.org/10.1177/1088868316685018

Kealy, D., & Ogrodniczuk, J. S. (2011). Narcissistic interpersonal problems in clinical practice. Harvard review of psychiatry, 19(6), 290-301.

Kernberg, O. F. (1970). Factors in the psychoanalytic treatment of narcissistic personalities. *Journal of the American Psychoanalytic Association*, 18, 51-85. http://dx.doi.org/10.1177/000306517001800103

Kernberg, O. F. (2014) An Overview of the Treatment of Severe Narcissistic Pathology. *International Journal of Psychoanalysis* 95:865-888

Kjærvik, S. L., & Bushman, B. J. (2021). The link between narcissism and aggression: A meta-analytic review. *Psychological bulletin, 147*(5), 477.

Kohut, H. (2009). The restoration of the self. Chicago, IL: University of Chicago Press. (Original work published 1977) http://dx.doi.org/10.7208/chicago/ 9780226450155.001.0001

Masterson, J. F. (2013). *The real self: A developmental, self and object relations approach.* Routledge.

Ogden, T. (1979). On projective identification. *International Journal of Psycho-Analysis*, 6:357-373.

Oliveira, C.M., & Levine, T.R. (2008). Lie acceptability: A construct and measure. *Communication Research Reports*, 25(4), 282–288.

Porges, S. W. (2009). The polyvagal theory: new insights into adaptive reactions of the autonomic nervous system. *Cleveland Clinic journal of medicine*, 76(Suppl 2), S86.

Reid, J., & Kealy, D. (2024). Features of Pathogenic Beliefs in the Context of Childhood Maltreatment: Implications for Therapeutic Empathy. *Studies in Clinical Social Work: Transforming Practice, Education and Research*, 94(2), 91-108.

Schwartz, R. C., & Sweezy, M. (2019). *Internal family systems therapy*. Guilford Publications.

Tronick, E. Z., & Gianino, A. (1986). Interactive mismatch and repair: Challenges to the coping infant. *Zero to Three*, 6(3), 1–6.

Wallace, D. F. (2009). *This is water*. Little, Brown & Company.

Weinberg, I., & Ronningstam, E. (2022). Narcissistic personality disorder: Progress in understanding and treatment. Focus, 20(4), 368-377.